WINDOWS® 3.1

Sarah E. Hutchinson
Stacey C. Sawyer
Glen J. Coulthard

THE IRWIN ADVANTAGE SERIES
FOR COMPUTER EDUCATION

♦

IRWIN

Burr Ridge, Illinois
Boston, Massachusetts
Sydney, Australia

Printed in the United States of America.

ISBN 0-256-13521-5

Windows is a registered trademark of Microsoft Corporation.

14 15 16 17 ML 0 9 8 7 6 5

CONTENTS

SESSION 2
WINDOWS 3.1: WORKING WITH WINDOWS   33

SESSION 3
WINDOWS 3.1: MANAGING YOUR WORK   65

SESSION 4
WINDOWS 3.1: USING WRITE AND OTHER ACCESSORY
PROGRAMS   111

SESSION 5
WINDOWS 3.1: INCREASING YOUR PRODUCTIVITY 153

USING THIS GUIDE

This tutorial is one in a series of learning guides that lead you through the most popular microcomputer software programs available. Concepts, skills, and procedures are grouped into session topics and are presented in a logical and structured manner. Commands and procedures are introduced using hands-on examples, and you are encouraged to perform the steps along with the guide. Although you may turn directly to a later session, be aware that some sessions require, or at least assume, that you have completed the previous sessions. For maximum benefit, you should work through the short-answer and hands-on exercises appearing at the end of each session.

The exercises and examples in this guide use several standard conventions to indicate menu options, keystroke combinations, and command instructions.

MENU INSTRUCTIONS

In Windows 3.1, all Menu bar options and pull-down menu commands have an underlined or highlighted letter in each option. When you need to execute a command from the Menu bar--the row of menu choices across the top of the screen--the tutorial's instruction line separates the Menu bar option from the command with a comma. For example, the command for quitting Windows 3.1 is shown as:

   CHOOSE: File, Exit

This instruction tells you to choose the File option on the Menu bar and then to choose the Exit command from the File pull-down menu. The actual steps for choosing a menu command are discussed later in this guide.

KEYSTROKES AND KEYSTROKE COMBINATIONS

When two keys must be pressed together, the tutorial's instruction line shows the keys joined with a plus sign (+). For example, you execute a command from the Windows Menu bar by holding down the [Alt] key and then pressing the key with the underlined or highlighted letter of the desired command.

To illustrate this type of keystroke combination, the following statement shows how to access the File menu option.

PRESS: [Alt]+f

In this instruction, you first press the [Alt] key and then hold it down while you press the f key. Once both keys have been pressed, they are then immediately released.

COMMAND INSTRUCTIONS

This guide indicates with a special typeface data that you are required to type in yourself. For example:

TYPE: George Washington

When you are required to enter unique information, such as the current date or your name, the instructions appear in *italics*. The following instruction directs you to type your name in place of the actual words: "your name."

TYPE: *your name*

Instructions that use general directions rather than a specific option or command name appear italicized in the regular typeface:

SELECT: *a different pattern for the chart*

WINDOWS 3.1: FUNDAMENTALS

Throughout the past decade, software developers have produced powerful business- and task-oriented software for corporate users. Unfortunately, many of these programs were difficult to learn and spawned the need for technical gurus in organizations. To sell home and office software today, however, the word "friendly" is more important than "powerful." Microsoft Windows has helped create this new market focus. In this first session, you are introduced to Windows and explore the reasons why over 10 million copies have been sold since 1990.

PREVIEW

When you have completed this session, you will be able to:

Explain the advantages of Microsoft Windows.
•
Load Microsoft Windows 3.1.
•
Describe the components of the Windows screen.
•
Move, size, maximize, and minimize windows.
•
Automatically arrange windows.
•
Choose commands from the Menu bar and dialog boxes.
•
Exit Microsoft Windows 3.1.

Why Is This Session Important?
What Is Windows?
      The Windows Environment
      Program Manager
      File Manager
      Print Manager
      Accessory Programs
      Task Manager
      TrueType Fonts
      Multimedia Applications
      Windows NT
The Windows Advantage
Working with Microsoft Windows
      How the Mouse Is Used
      How the Keyboard Is Used
Starting Windows
The Guided Tour
      Application Window
      Document Window
Executing Programs and Commands
      Menu Bar
      Dialog Box
Manipulating Windows
      Sizing a Window
      Moving a Window
      Organizing Windows
      Selecting Windows
Exiting Windows
Summary
      Command Summary
Key Terms
Exercises
      Short Answer
      Hands-On

WHY IS THIS SESSION IMPORTANT?

This guide leads you step-by-step through Microsoft Windows 3.1. Developed by Microsoft Corporation, Windows brings a graphical, user-friendly interface to your computer system that makes learning computers easier. Windows enables users at all levels to take full advantage of today's sophisticated microprocessors. By the completion of this guide, you will have the fundamental skills for working in the Windows environment.

In Session 1, you learn about Windows' features and how to manipulate application and document windows. The Program Manager, Control Panel, and Print Manager programs are introduced in Session 2 for customizing your work area and setting up printers. To perform file and disk management in Windows, you use File Manager, which is introduced in Session 3. In Session 4, you learn how to use some of the accessory programs that are provided with Windows, including the Write word processor, the Paintbrush drawing program, and Solitaire. To increase your productivity and optimize Windows' performance, Session 5 discusses multitasking, exchanging information among applications, recording macros, and managing memory.

WHAT IS WINDOWS?

Microsoft Windows is an *operating environment* that enhances DOS with a **graphical user interface** or GUI (pronounced "gooey") that lets you launch programs and manage files using a mouse. Windows is often referred to incorrectly as an *operating system*. An operating system controls the resources of the computer and the basic input and output operations. DOS is the operating system for the majority of personal computers; other operating systems include OS/2, Unix, and CP/M.

Microsoft first announced Windows in 1985. However, the product did not gain widespread commercial success until the release of Windows 3.0 in May 1990. With Windows 3.0, Microsoft enhanced the user interface and memory support and improved the overall performance of the program. In the spring of 1992, Microsoft released Windows 3.1.

THE WINDOWS ENVIRONMENT

Many types of software enable users to perform a wide range of processing tasks. Each category of software—for example, word processing, spreadsheet, database, and graphics—provides the user with a different set of capabilities. To satisfy all processing requirements, many personal computer owners use more than one type of software program. Unfortunately, each program has its own set of menus, commands, and procedures. As a result, some users find that microcomputers are difficult and frustrating to use because learning one software program does not help them in using other programs.

One of Microsoft's mandates in developing Windows was to make computers easier to use. To this end, all Windows applications incorporate a common menu system and share many of the same commands and procedures. But this also requires that personal computer owners purchase different versions of their favorite software applications. Currently, software retail stores carry two versions of the most popular products, like Lotus 1-2-3 for DOS and Lotus 1-2-3 for Windows, WordPerfect for DOS and WordPerfect for Windows, and the list goes on.

With standardized menus, Windows users become more productive because they do not have to memorize a new set of commands for each application. In addition, Windows enables you to run multiple applications at the same time, so you do not have to exit one program to start another. As well, with Windows File Manager and support for running your favorite DOS applications, you may never again need to face the C:\> prompt.

PROGRAM MANAGER

In Microsoft Windows, Program Manager acts as the main menu for the programs on your computer. You organize applications into groups that suit your personal work style and launch applications such as File Manager, Print Manager, and Control Panel. Program Manager is the central management program for Windows; without it you cannot use other application programs. When you close Program Manager, you also close Microsoft Windows.

Program Manager is discussed in Session 2 of this guide.

FILE MANAGER

Before Windows, most file and disk management tasks were performed from the DOS command line. To copy a file or format a disk, you entered a cryptic DOS command that resembled a line from the "Computer Programmer's Handbook." If you missed one space or mixed up the order of words in the command, the computer retorted with a curt and unforgiving message. With File Manager, Windows takes the frustration out of managing your work and disk storage areas.

File Manager performs the following file and disk management functions:

- Organizes and manipulates files, directories, and disks
- Copies, moves, renames, and deletes files
- Creates, renames, and removes directories
- Formats, copies, and labels hard disks and floppy diskettes
- Launches application programs

In Session 3, you practice managing files and disks using File Manager.

PRINT MANAGER

When you print a document in Windows, the document is sent to an intermediary program called Print Manager. Print Manager allows you to send several documents to the printer while you continue to work in an application program. Without Windows and Print Manager, you must wait for the printer to finish before using the computer. Print Manager therefore increases your productivity by reducing your idle time.

Print Manager performs the following functions:

- Stores documents sent to the printer in a print queue
- Manages the priority and order of printing documents
- Pauses, resumes, and deletes print jobs

Print Manager is discussed in the latter part of Session 2.

ACCESSORY PROGRAMS

Included in the Windows package are several accessory programs, ranging from personal productivity tools to advanced utility programs. For example, Windows provides a clock program that enables you to display the current time on the screen as you work with other application programs. Windows also provides a notepad program that lets you quickly create, save, and print short lists or reminders. In addition to these smaller programs, Windows provides a word processing program called Write, a paint program called Paintbrush, and a communications program called Terminal.

Several accessory programs are introduced in Session 4.

TASK MANAGER

Windows is a multitasking environment that allows several programs to be running at the same time. For example, you can run the Windows Clock program, Notepad program, Write word processor, and Terminal communications package at the same time. You use Task Manager to control and manage the applications that are running in memory.

Session 5 discusses multitasking under Windows and Task Manager.

TRUETYPE FONTS

One of the more interesting features of Windows is the ability to work with different typefaces using a **WYSIWYG** (What You See Is What You Get) display. With WYSIWYG, what you see on the screen is what you will get at the printer, so you can try different typefaces to enhance a document's presentation quality and communicability. A **typeface** is a style of print. (Note: Microsoft Windows applications use the terms *typeface* and *font* interchangeably. Traditionally, however, a **font** is defined as all the symbols and characters of a typeface for a particular point size.) Windows standardizes different typefaces for applications and printers using a feature called **TrueType**.

TrueType allows you to manipulate scalable typefaces to produce onscreen fonts that closely match printed output. Being scalable, TrueType fonts enable you to select any typeface at almost any point size and have Windows immediately display a crisp WYSIWYG image of the type onscreen. Windows 3.1 includes 14 TrueType fonts, and you can purchase additional fonts as desired.

MULTIMEDIA APPLICATIONS

Windows 3.1 enables you to use new and exciting technology, including multimedia applications—audio tracks, animation, and photographic images. With high-resolution graphics and audio capabilities, personal computers are becoming used more for corporate presentation, education, and entertainment applications. Windows 3.1 supports two types of audio: MIDI (musical instrument digital interface) and waveform (also called digital audio). MIDI enables you to create synthesized sounds, while waveform records and plays sounds like a tape recorder. To use the special multimedia capabilities of Windows 3.1, you require special hardware such as an audio board, CD-ROM, or a personal computing system that meets Multimedia PC (MPC) Specification 1.0.

WINDOWS NT

Microsoft Windows NT differs significantly from Windows 3.1 in several areas. Windows NT is a full-featured 32-bit operating system, similar to OS/2, and is marketed for high-level computing needs. The minimum system configuration for Windows NT requires an 80386 computer, 8 MB of RAM, and a large hard disk. Windows 3.1, on the other hand, is produced for the average personal computer user and requires a minimum system configuration of an 80286 computer with 1 MB of RAM. This guide focuses on the capabilities and features of Windows 3.1 only.

THE WINDOWS ADVANTAGE

Windows provides a common environment for your applications and, therefore, improves your productivity. You can use a pointing device called a **mouse** to select from **icons** (pictures that represent programs or functions) rather than typing lengthy commands. With a standardized mouse and keyboard interface, the knowledge you learn from using one Windows application helps you to use other Windows applications.

Some advantages of working in the Windows environment are these:

1. *The ability to run more than one application at a time.*
   Windows is a **multitasking** environment whereby more than one application or program may be running at the same time. This feature is

especially important for electronic mail, modem, or fax programs that must be loaded in memory to inform you of incoming messages.

2. *The ability to copy and move information among applications.*
    Windows provides a program called the Clipboard to copy and move information within an application or among applications. Because more than one application can be running at the same time, it is very easy to copy information from a spreadsheet to the Clipboard, and then paste the information from the Clipboard into a word processing document.

3. *The ability to link or embed objects from one application into another.*
    The latest products being released for Microsoft Windows have the ability to integrate applications using a feature called OLE (pronounced "Olé") or Object Linking and Embedding. This feature enables you to embed an object created using one application into another application, and facilitates sharing and manipulating information. An object may be a document, worksheet, chart, picture, or even a sound recording. OLE is discussed further in Session 5.

4. *The ability to display on the screen what you will get at the printer.*
    This feature is called WYSIWYG and allows different fonts, borders, and graphics to be displayed on the screen at all times. Most DOS programs provide a print preview feature but do not display the true WYSIWYG capabilities of Windows programs.

5. *The ability to enhance documents with multiple fonts and graphics.*
    In Windows, you not only can display fonts and graphics at all times, but you can choose from multiple typefaces, font sizes, and graphic images to insert into documents.

The primary disadvantage of working in the Windows environment is that the program requires a powerful computer to maintain a reasonable processing speed. The system requirements, from a practical point of view, are a 386-based computer with 2 MB of RAM and 6 MB of free disk space. To improve the response time in Windows, increase RAM size and use a disk caching software utility program. For further discussion on increasing the performance of Windows on your computer, refer to the Speeding Up Windows section in Session 5.

WORKING WITH MICROSOFT WINDOWS

Microsoft Windows is a graphical program. To fully appreciate its functionality, you should become familiar with certain mouse actions. Instructions in this guide attempt to list both the mouse and keyboard methods for performing commands and procedures. You should try the instructions for each method and decide for yourself which you prefer. This section provides some information on how the mouse and keyboard are used in Windows 3.1.

HOW THE MOUSE IS USED

The mouse is an essential tool for working in the Windows environment. Although it is possible to use Windows with only a keyboard, much of the program's basic design revolves around the use of a mouse. Although your mouse may have two or three buttons, Windows primarily uses the left mouse button for selecting items and commands.

The mouse actions used in Windows are click, double-click, and drag:

- Click

  Press down and release the left mouse button quickly. Clicking is used to position the cursor or insertion symbol, to select commands, and to choose options from a dialog box.

- Double-Click

  Press down and release the left mouse button twice in rapid succession. Double-clicking is often used to select and execute a program or procedure.

- Drag

  Press down and hold the left mouse button as you move the mouse pointer across the screen. When the mouse pointer reaches the desired location, release the mouse button. Dragging is used to move icons or windows, or to select text.

You may notice that the mouse pointer changes shape as you move the mouse over different parts of the screen. Each mouse pointer shape has its own purpose and may provide you with important information. As shown in Table 1.1, there are many mouse shapes that may appear in Windows.

Table 1.1	*Symbol*	*Name*	*Description*
Mouse pointer shapes	☜	arrow	Used to choose menu items, make selections from dialog boxes, or move windows
	⧖	hourglass	Tells you that Windows is occupied and to wait until it is finished
	I	I-beam	Used to modify and edit text, and to position the cursor in text boxes
	☞	hand	In the Help window, the hand is used to select topics and jump terms (discussed in Session 2)

As you proceed through this guide, other mouse shapes will be explained as they appear.

How the Keyboard Is Used

Aside from being the primary input device for entering data, the keyboard offers shortcut methods for performing commands and procedures. For example, several menu commands have shortcut key combinations listed to the right of the command in the pull-down menu. Therefore, you can perform a command by simply pressing the shortcut keys rather than accessing the Menu bar. Many of these shortcut key combinations are available throughout Windows applications.

Starting Windows

Because Microsoft Windows requires a hard disk, this session assumes that you are working on a computer with DOS and Windows loaded on the hard disk drive. In most cases, the hard disk of a personal computer is drive C:. The Windows program is stored in a directory on the hard disk called \WINDOWS, much like having a reserved drawer in a filing cabinet.

Before using Windows, you must turn on the computer and load DOS. Perform the following steps on your computer.

1. Turn on the power switches to the computer and monitor. The C:\> prompt or a menu appears announcing that your computer has successfully loaded DOS. (<u>Note</u>: Your computer may automatically load Microsoft Windows when it is started. If you see the Microsoft Windows logo appear on the screen, move on to step 3.)

2. To start Microsoft Windows from the C:\> prompt:
   TYPE: `win`
   PRESS: (Enter)
   After a few seconds, the Windows logo appears on the screen followed by the Program Manager window (Figure 1.1). (<u>Note</u>: The icons in your Program Manager window may not be exactly the same as in Figure 1.1; the icons represent the programs stored on your hard disk.)

Figure 1.1

The Microsoft
Windows Program
Manager

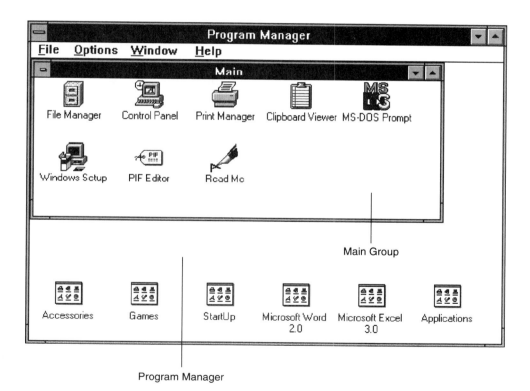

Main Group

Program Manager

....

Quick Reference   To start Windows from the C:\> prompt:
Starting Windows   TYPE: win
                        PRESS: (Enter)

....

THE GUIDED TOUR

Software programs designed for Microsoft Windows, such as Word for Windows, Excel, and PageMaker, have many similarities in screen design and layout. Each application program runs in its own rectangular area on the screen called an **application window**. In an application program, you create your work in a **document window**. This section introduces the components of application and document windows.

When you first load Windows 3.1, Program Manager appears in an application window on the Desktop. The **Desktop** provides the background screen for all application windows. Inside the Program Manager window, there are several **group icons** and **group windows**. A group window is a special type of document window that contains **program icons**. To launch an application, you open the appropriate group window and then select the application's program icon. If you have just installed Windows on your computer, the Main group window appears in the top left corner of the application window. The Main group window contains general system applications, such as File Manager, Print Manager, and Control Panel.

APPLICATION WINDOW

Application windows, such as Program Manager in Figure 1.2, have the following characteristics: Title bar, Menu bar, Control menu, and Minimize and Maximize buttons. In an application window, you can open multiple document windows simultaneously. Document windows contain the actual work that you create and store on the disk.

Figure 1.2

Application window

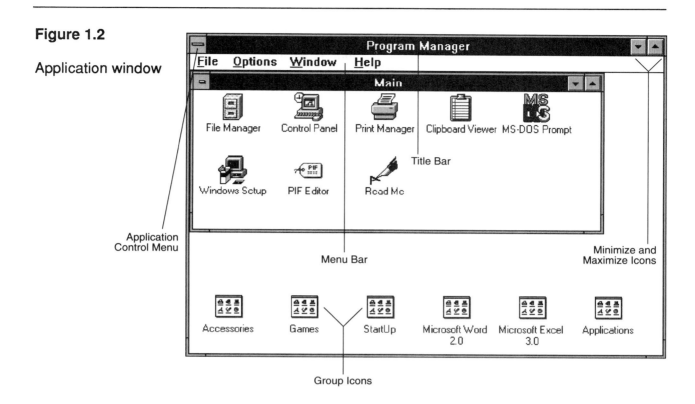

TITLE BAR   The Title bar, located at the top of a window, contains the name of the application or current document. In Figure 1.2, "Program Manager" appears in the application Title bar and "Main" appears in the document or group Title bar. The Title bar also differentiates an active window, which has a solid Title bar, from a nonactive window. Commands that you select from an application's Menu bar affect only the active window. Using a mouse, you can move a window by dragging its Title bar.

MENU BAR   The Menu bar appears on the second line from the top in an application window and contains commands for manipulating items in the window. The Menu bar is accessed by holding down the (Alt) key and pressing the underlined letter of the desired command, or by clicking on the command using the mouse. When activated, the Menu bar displays a pull-down menu. To leave the Menu bar, press (Esc) twice.

CONTROL MENU   Every application window and document window has a Control menu that appears as a small horizontal bar in the top left-hand corner. Accessed by holding down the (Alt) key and pressing the Space Bar, the application Control menu is used to manipulate a window using the keyboard. The Control menu for a document window is activated by holding down the [Alt] key and pressing the Hyphen key. To close an application or document window, select the Close command from the pull-down menu or simply double-click the Control menu. For example, you can quit Windows by double-clicking the Program Manager's Control menu. To leave the Control Menu, press [Esc] twice.

MINIMIZE AND MAXIMIZE ICONS   The Minimize and Maximize icons are located in the top right-hand corner of an application or document window. These triangular-shaped icons control the size and display of a window using a mouse. Applications are often minimized from view when they are not currently needed but must remain running. Minimized program icons appear along the bottom row of the Desktop.

DOCUMENT WINDOW

Document windows provide the work space for an application. When there is more information available than can appear in the document window at a single time, scroll bars are displayed at the right or bottom borders. You use the scroll bars to move around a document window by clicking the arrow heads at either end of a scroll bar or by dragging the "Thumb" or scroll box. Figure 1.3 shows the Control menu, program icons, and Minimize and Maximize icons for the Main group window.

Figure 1.3

Main group or
document window

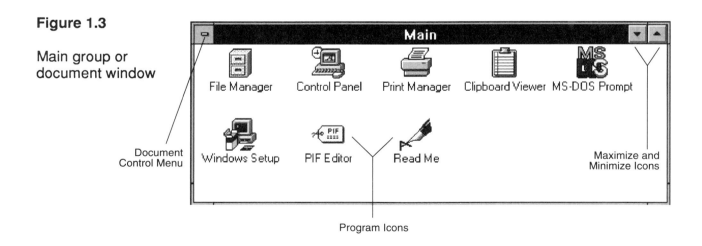

Document
Control Menu

Program Icons

EXECUTING PROGRAMS AND COMMANDS

In Windows, you launch application programs by double-clicking program icons that appear in group windows. Once an application is running, you perform most procedures by issuing commands from its Menu bar and choosing options in dialog boxes.

MENU BAR

Commands are grouped together on a Menu bar, located at the top of an application window. To execute a command, you first select an option from the Menu bar and then choose a command from the pull-down menu. The commands on a pull-down menu that are not available for selection appear dimmed. A check mark beside a command means that the command is currently active.

To access the menu and execute a command using a mouse, click once on the Menu bar option to display the pull-down menu. From the pull-down menu, click once on the command you want to execute. Another way to select a command is to click on the menu option and then drag the mouse pointer down the pull-down menu to the desired command. When the command is highlighted, release the mouse button to execute it.

To execute a command using the keyboard, press and hold down the (Alt) key and then tap the underlined letter of the desired option on the Menu bar. When the pull-down menu is displayed, press the underlined letter of the command you want to execute. Commands appear in this guide in the following form: File, Open, where File is the Menu bar option and Open is the command to be selected from the pull-down menu.

You can cancel a selection once you are in the Menu bar by pressing the (Esc) key twice. To cancel a menu selection using a mouse, move the pointer off the menu item and release the mouse button. If you have already executed a command that displays a dialog box, select the Cancel command button to abort the procedure.

Perform the following steps.

1. To choose the File menu option using the keyboard:
   PRESS: (Alt)+f

2. To browse the pull-down menus:
    PRESS: → several times

3. Continue pressing → until the pull-down menu returns to the File
    option.

4. To exit the menu:
    PRESS: (Esc) twice

DIALOG BOX

A dialog box is a common mechanism in Windows applications for
collecting information before processing a command or instruction
(Figure 1.4). An ellipsis (...) following a command on a pull-down menu
means a dialog box appears when the command is selected. Dialog boxes
are also used to display messages or to ask for confirmation of commands.

Figure 1.4

A dialog box

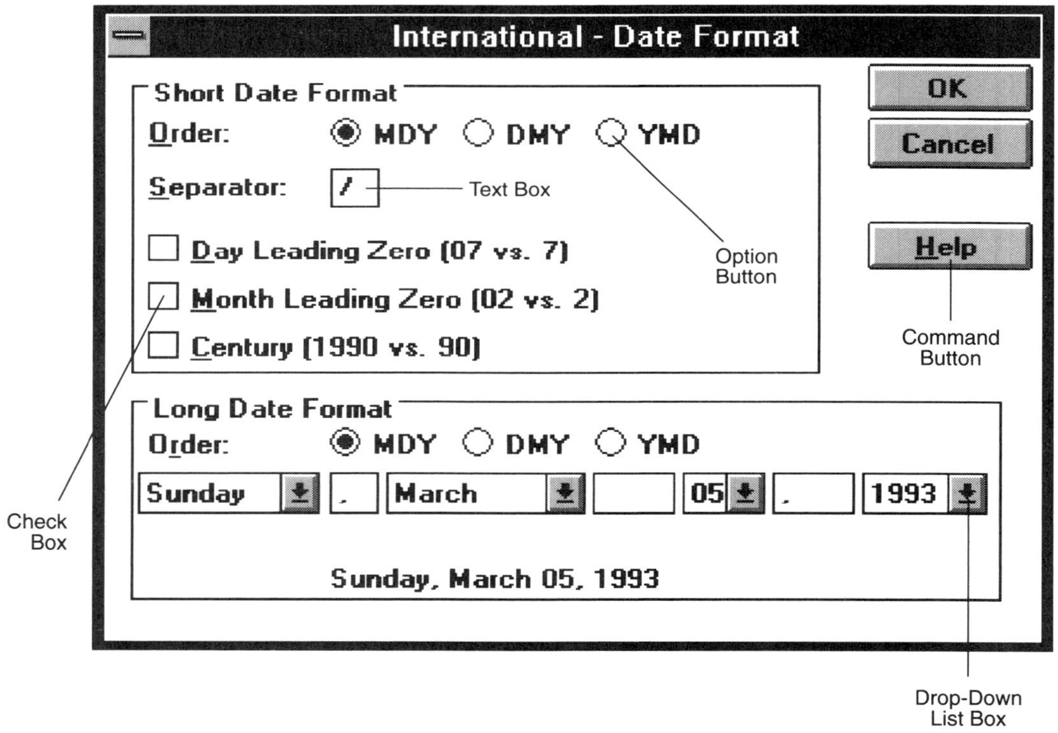

A dialog box uses several methods for collecting information, including list boxes, drop-down list boxes, text boxes, check boxes, option buttons, and command buttons. You can access an item in the dialog box using the mouse or by pressing (Tab) to move clockwise and (Shift)+(Tab) to move counterclockwise around the dialog box.

Study Table 1.2 and Figure 1.4 on the common elements found in dialog boxes. In the following sessions, you use dialog boxes to choose printers, customize the Desktop, manage files, and to perform many other tasks.

Table 1.2	*Element*	*Description*
Parts of a dialog box	List box	A scrollable list of choices; shows all choices
	Drop-down list box	A scrollable list of choices; shows selected choice only
	Text box	A box for collecting typed information
	Check box	An option that can be turned on or off
	Option button	One option selected from a group of related options
	Command button	A button that executes an action when selected

MANIPULATING WINDOWS

This section introduces methods for sizing, moving, and organizing windows. Similar to shuffling pages on your desk, you position application windows on the Windows Desktop to work more efficiently.

SIZING A WINDOW

You size an application or document window by dragging its borders using the mouse, or by selecting the Size command from the window's Control menu. Although you can drag any border, the corners of a window frame allow you to size a window both horizontally and vertically. In most cases, changing the size of a window does not affect the contents of the window.

You can also maximize or minimize a window by clicking on the icons in the top right-hand corner or by choosing commands from the window's Control menu. The following situations occur when maximizing or minimizing windows:

- Maximizing an application window expands the window to fill the entire screen—no part of the Desktop remains visible.
- Maximizing a document window expands the window to fill its application window. The Title bar for a maximized document window melds with the Title bar of the application window. The Control menu for a maximized document window appears beneath the application Control menu and to the left of the Menu bar.
- When a window is maximized, its Maximize icon ([▲]) is replaced with a Restore icon ([‡]) for restoring the window back to its original size.
- Minimizing an application window reduces the window to an icon on the Desktop.
- Minimizing a document window usually reduces the window to an icon in the application window.
- When a window is minimized to an icon, you restore it to a window by double-clicking on the icon or by highlighting it and pressing (**Enter**).

To practice sizing windows, perform the following steps.

1. To minimize the Main group window:
    CLICK: Minimize icon ([▾]) for the Main group window
    Position the mouse pointer over the icon and click the left mouse button once. Ensure that you do not click the Minimize icon for the Program Manager. (Note: If the Main group window is already minimized to an icon in Program Manager, proceed to the next step.)

2. To open the Main group window from an icon:
    DOUBLE-CLICK: Main group icon
    Position the mouse pointer over the icon with "Main" in its title and then press and release the left mouse button twice in rapid succession.

3. To open the Accessories group window:
    CLICK: Accessories group icon once
    The Control menu appears for the group icon.

4. CHOOSE: Restore from the Control menu
    To choose the Restore command, you click on the command using the mouse or press the cursor-movement keys to highlight the command and then press (**Enter**). The Accessories group window appears in the Program Manager window.

5. To minimize the Accessories group window using the menu:
   PRESS: (Alt)+Hyphen
   The Accessories Control menu is displayed.

6. CHOOSE: Close
   The Accessories group window is minimized to an icon. (Note: You can also choose Minimize to minimize the group window to an icon.)

7. To increase the width of the Main group window, first position the mouse pointer over the right vertical border. The mouse pointer changes to a double-headed arrow when positioned correctly.

8. CLICK: left mouse button and hold it down
   DRAG: mouse pointer to the right by approximately 1 inch
   You should notice that a shadow of the border frame is moved with the mouse pointer.

9. Release the left mouse button to complete the sizing operation.

10. To decrease the width of the Main group window, position the mouse pointer over the right vertical border until the pointer changes shape.

11. CLICK: left mouse button and hold it down
    DRAG: mouse pointer to the left until the window is 1 inch wide

12. Release the left mouse button. Your screen should appear similar to Figure 1.5.

Figure 1.5

Sizing the Main
group window

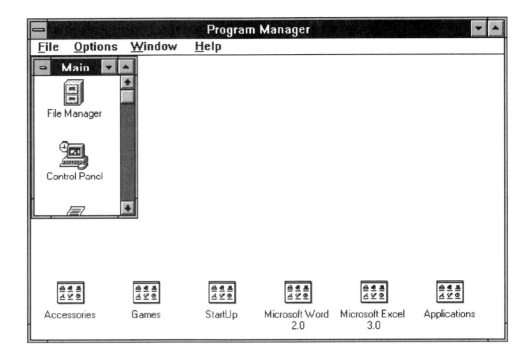

13. To move around the window using the mouse:
     CLICK: arrows at the top and bottom of the vertical scroll bar

14. To move around the window using the Thumb or scroll box, first
     position the mouse pointer on the Thumb box.

15. CLICK: left mouse button and hold it down
     DRAG: mouse pointer and Thumb box along the scroll bar

16. Release the mouse button.

17. To resize the Main group window using the keyboard:
     PRESS: (Alt)+Hyphen

18. CHOOSE: Size

19. PRESS: (→) several times until the window returns to its original size
     (Note: You can also hold down the (→) key to move large distances,
     rather than pressing it multiple times.)

20. PRESS: (Enter) to lock the new window size

....

Quick Reference   1. Position the mouse pointer on the window's border until the mouse
Sizing Windows   pointer changes to a double-headed arrow.
                       2. Press the left mouse button and hold it down.
                       3. Drag the window frame to increase or decrease its size.
                       4. Release the left mouse button to complete the sizing operation.

....

MOVING A WINDOW

You move an application or document window by dragging its Title bar
using the mouse, or by selecting the Move command from the window's
Control menu. Although you can move application windows anywhere on
the Desktop, document windows are limited to their application window.
In other words, you cannot move a document or group window outside of
its application window.

Perform the following steps.

1. Position the mouse pointer on the Main group window's Title bar.

2. To move the window:
    CLICK: left mouse button and hold it down
    DRAG: mouse pointer towards the bottom right-hand corner
    Notice that a shadow of the window frame is moved.

3. When it is positioned correctly, release the left mouse button.

4. To move the window using the keyboard:
    PRESS: (Alt)+Hyphen
    CHOOSE: Move

5. PRESS: (←) multiple times
    PRESS: (↑) multiple times

6. When you finish returning the window to its original location:
    PRESS: (Enter) to lock the window's position

....
Quick Reference   1. Position the mouse pointer on the window's Title bar.
Moving Windows   2. Press the left mouse button and hold it down.
   3. Drag the window frame to a new location.
   4. Release the left mouse button to complete the move operation.

....

ORGANIZING WINDOWS

In addition to arranging windows by moving each window individually, you can automatically arrange all open windows using the Window menu option. To layer the open windows in the Program Manager application window, choose Window, Cascade from the menu or press (Shift)+(F5). The active window is displayed on top of the other windows in a cascaded arrangement. To display all open windows in a floor tile pattern, choose Window, Tile or press (Shift)+(F4). The active window is placed in the top left-hand corner and the other windows are placed next to each other until the application window is filled.

Perform the following steps.

1. Open all the group windows by double-clicking on the group icons. (Note: If an open window hides a group icon, you can move it using the mouse or choose the group from the Window pull-down menu.)

2. To layer the open windows:
CHOOSE: Window, Cascade
This instruction tells you to choose the Window option on the Menu bar. Once the pull-down menu appears, you choose the Cascade command. To do this using a keyboard, press (Alt)+w to display the pull-down menu, and then press c to choose Cascade. Using a mouse, you simply click on the commands. Your screen should now appear similar to Figure 1.6.

Figure 1.6

Cascading open
group windows

3. To tile the open windows:
   CHOOSE: Window, Tile

4. To quickly cascade the open windows:
   PRESS: Shift + F5

5. To quickly tile the open windows:
   PRESS: Shift + F4
   Your screen should appear similar to Figure 1.7.

Figure 1.7

Tiling open group
windows

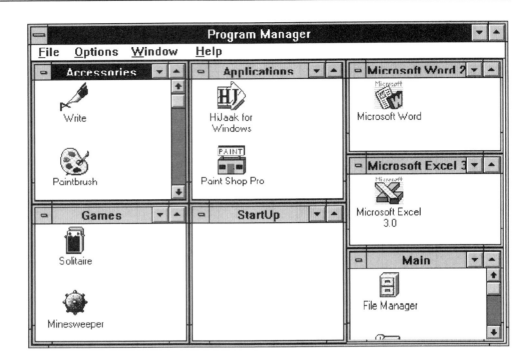

Quick Reference   •   To arrange windows in a layered format, choose Window, Cascade
Arranging   from the menu or press Shift+F5.
Windows   •   To arrange windows in a tiled format, choose Window, Tile from the
                             menu or press Shift+F4.

SELECTING WINDOWS

Before issuing a command from the Menu bar, you must first select the
window to be affected by the command. The selected window is called the
active window. To select an application or document window using the
mouse, you simply click on a visible part of the window. Using the
keyboard, you press Ctrl+Tab or Ctrl+F6 to cycle through the open
document or group windows. To cycle through the open applications, you
press Alt+Tab or use Task Manager. Switching among open application
windows is discussed in Session 5.

Perform the following steps to cycle through the open group windows.

1.   CHOOSE: Window, Cascade

2. To cycle through the open group windows:
   PRESS: Ctrl+Tab multiple times
   Notice that the Title bar changes as each group window becomes active.

3. To continue cycling through the open group windows:
   PRESS: Ctrl+F6

....
Quick Reference   To select a document or group window, press Ctrl+Tab or Ctrl+F6
Selecting the   to cycle through the open windows in an application window.
Active Window
....

EXITING WINDOWS

You should always exit Windows before turning off the computer. If you have arranged the group windows in Program Manager, you can save their new positions using the Options, Save Settings on Exit command. When a check mark appears beside this menu command, the option is active and will save the appearance of Program Manager whenever you exit Windows. Once you have organized the group windows and saved your preferences for Program Manager, you should turn this command off so that the saved settings become the default start-up settings.

Perform the following steps.

1. To save the window positions in Program Manager when you exit, ensure that a check mark appears beside the Save Settings on Exit command in the Options pull-down menu:
   CHOOSE: Options, Save Settings on Exit
   If there is a check mark beside the option already, then you need not perform this step.

2. To retain the original startup settings and discard the current window positions, ensure that no check mark appears beside the Save Settings on Exit command:
   CHOOSE: Options, Save Settings on Exit again

CAUTION: Ensure that there is not a check mark beside the §ave Settings on Exit command before proceeding to the next step. You do not want to save the positions of the open group windows that appear in the Program Manager window.

3. To exit Windows:
    CHOOSE: Eile, Exit Windows
    (Note: You can also double-click the Program Manager's Control menu to close Windows.)

4. PRESS: [Enter] or CLICK: OK

....

Quick Reference   1. To save the Program Manager settings and window positions,
Exiting Windows   choose the Options, §ave Settings on Exit command before exiting
                            Windows. The command is active when a check mark appears
                            beside the command on the pull-down menu.
                        2. To exit Windows, choose Eile, Exit Windows or double-click on the
                            Program Manager Control menu.
                        3. Press [Enter] or click on OK.

....

SUMMARY

Microsoft Windows is not an operating system; it's an operating environment that works with DOS to make the computer easier to use. This session introduced you to the advantages of working in the Windows environment. The primary components of Windows include Program Manager, File Manager, Print Manager, Task Manager, and several accessory programs.

In the latter half of the session, you loaded Microsoft Windows 3.1 and went on a guided tour of the main parts of the Windows screen. You sized, moved, and arranged document or group windows using the mouse and keyboard. You also cycled through open group windows in Program Manager using [Ctrl]+[Tab] and [Ctrl]+[F6]. The session concluded with a section on exiting Windows and saving the settings for Program Manager.

Many of the commands and procedures introduced in this session appear in the Command Summary (Table 1.3).

Table 1.3	*Command*	*Description*
Command Summary	<u>W</u>indow, <u>C</u>ascade	Layer open windows with the active window on top
	<u>W</u>indow, <u>T</u>ile	Arrange open windows in a floor tile format with the active window in the top left-hand corner
	<u>O</u>ptions, <u>S</u>ave Settings on Exit	Save the Program Manager settings and window positions
	<u>F</u>ile, E<u>x</u>it Windows	Exit Microsoft Windows 3.1

KEY TERMS

active window   The document or application window that is currently selected; commands affect the active window only.

application window   In Windows, each running application program appears in its own application window. These windows can be sized and moved anywhere on the Windows Desktop.

Desktop   The background screen for Windows where you place applications and organize your work.

document window   In Windows, each open document, whether a worksheet or letter, appears in its own document window. These windows can be sized and moved anywhere within the application window.

font   Traditionally, all of the symbols and characters of a typeface for a particular point size. Windows programs use the terms *font* and *typeface* interchangeably to mean all available sizes of a style of print.

graphical user interface   Software feature that allows the user to select menu options and choose icons to perform procedures; makes software easier to use, and typically employs a mouse.

group icons   In Program Manager, icons that represent program groups. To expand the program group into a group window, double-click on the group icon.

group windows   In Program Manager, document windows that contain and organize program item icons.

icon   Picture or symbol that represents a program group, application program, file, or other element on the Windows screen.

mouse   Handheld input device connected to a microcomputer by a cable; when the mouse is rolled across the desk or mouse pad, the cursor moves across the screen. A button on the mouse allows users to make menu selections and to issue commands.

multitasking   Activity in which more than one task or program is executed at a time. A small amount of each program is processed, and then the CPU moves to the remaining programs, one at a time, processing small parts of each.

program icons   In Program Manager, icons that represent application software programs. To execute an application, you double-click the application's program icon.

TrueType   Scalable font technology provided with Windows 3.1.

typeface   A style of print.

WYSIWYG   Acronym for *What You See Is What You Get.*

EXERCISES

SHORT ANSWER

1. What is an operating system?
2. What is the difference between a typeface and a font?
3. What is TrueType?
4. What are five advantages of using Windows, as listed in this session?
5. Describe three primary mouse movements in Windows.
6. Describe four common mouse pointer shapes.
7. What is the difference between an application and document window?
8. What happens when you maximize a document or group window?
9. What does it mean to *cascade* the open windows?
10. How can you save the group window positions in Program Manager when you exit Windows?

HANDS-ON

(<u>Note</u>: In the following exercises, you perform Windows commands using files located on the Advantage Diskette.)

1. This exercise practices manipulating windows in the Program Manager.
    a. Ensure that the Advantage Diskette is placed into drive A:.
    b. Start your computer and load DOS.
    c. Load Microsoft Windows 3.1 and wait for the Program Manager application window to appear.
    d. Close all open group windows using the keyboard:
        PRESS: (Alt)+Hyphen to display the Control menu for the active group window
        SELECT: <u>C</u>lose command
    e. Using the mouse, you will move each group icon from the bottom of the application window to the top—directly underneath the Menu bar. To begin, position the mouse pointer over a group icon.
    f. CLICK: left mouse button and hold it down
        DRAG: group icon to the top of the application window
    g. Release the mouse button.
    h. Repeat the drag operation for each icon until they are all lined up near the top of the application window.
    i. To move among the icons using the keyboard:
        PRESS: (Ctrl)+(Tab) several times
        Notice that the icon text is highlighted when an icon is selected.
    j. SELECT: Main group icon
        PRESS: (Enter)
    k. Using the mouse, size the Main group window to 2- by 2-inches by dragging the border at the bottom right corner.
    l. Position the mouse pointer on the Title bar of the Main group window.
    m. Move the window to the top right-hand corner of the Program Manager window by dragging the window frame.
    n. Using the keyboard, move the window into the center of the Program Manager window:
        PRESS: (Alt)+Hyphen
        CHOOSE: <u>M</u>ove
        PRESS: (↓) and (←) multiple times to position the Main group window
        PRESS: (Enter)
        Your screen should now appear similar to Figure 1.8.

Figure 1.8

Moving and sizing
the Main group
window

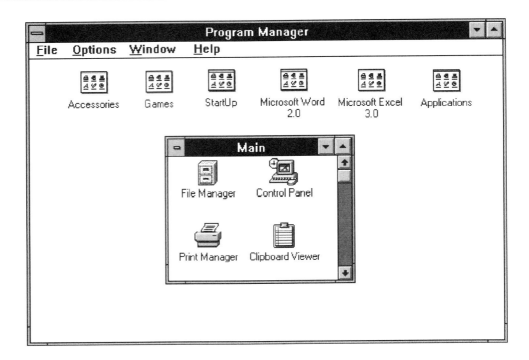

2. In this exercise, you maximize, minimize, cascade, and tile group
    windows in the Program Manager.
    a. Ensure that the Advantage Diskette is placed into drive A:.
    b. Ensure that the Main group window is the only open window in the
        Program Manager application window.
    c. Open the other group windows using the mouse:
        DOUBLE-CLICK: *all group icons*
    d. Cascade the open windows using the menu.
    e. Tile the open windows using the menu.
    f. PRESS: Ctrl+Tab to cycle through the open windows
    g. Close all the open group windows by double-clicking their Control
        menus. (Note: Make sure you do not double-click the Program
        Manager's Control menu.)
    h. Open the Main group window only.
    i. Maximize the Main group window:
        CLICK: Maximize icon in the Main group window
        Notice how the Main group window's Title bar melds with the
        Program Manager Title bar. Also note that there is a Restore icon
        in the top right-hand corner of the Program Manager window,
        immediately below the application window's Maximize icon.
    j. Restore the Main group to a window:
        CLICK: Restore icon
    k. Open up Accessories group window.

l. Open up StartUp group window.

m. Using the mouse, organize the open group windows to match the display in Figure 1.9.

Figure 1.9

Arranging open
group windows

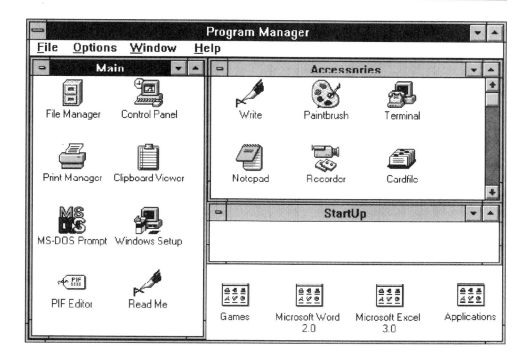

n. Close all the open group windows.

o. Exit Windows.

WINDOWS 3.1: WORKING WITH WINDOWS

Microsoft Windows keeps your computer desktop clean and organized. Similar to the way you work at your own desk, you can open a project's folder in Windows, temporarily set it aside to write a letter or calculate a bill, and then quickly return to the folder. With Windows you concentrate on getting things done, rather than learning how to do things. Windows makes adding new printers, customizing your work area, and managing application programs easy. This session teaches you how to use Program Manager, Control Panel, Print Manager, and the Help facility.

PREVIEW

When you have completed this session, you will be able to:

Name the program icons contained in the Main and
Accessories group windows.

•

Create an application group and program item.

•

Change the icon for a program item.

•

Change the color of the Windows screen.

•

Display a pattern or graphic on the Desktop.

•

Select and customize the default printer.

•

Use Print Manager to manipulate files in the print queue.

•

Retrieve context-sensitive help.

Why Is This Session Important?
Program Manager
    The StartUp Group
    Creating Groups and Program Items
    Changing Program Icons
    Deleting Groups and Program Items
Control Panel
    Choosing a Color Scheme
    Customizing the Desktop
    Using a Screen Saver
    Choosing a Printer
Print Manager
Getting Help
Summary
    Command Summary
Key Terms
Exercises
    Short Answer
    Hands-On

WHY IS THIS SESSION IMPORTANT?

This session introduces Program Manager, Control Panel, Print Manager, and the Windows Help facility. Program Manager manages application software programs, as demonstrated in Session 1. In this session, you review the program icons that appear in the Main and Accessories group windows. Control Panel enables you to customize the Windows Desktop and color schemes. Print Manager provides a queue for storing printed files to the disk, allowing you to continue working in an application while Windows manages the printing. Lastly, this session introduces the Windows Help facility for retrieving on-line help information.

In this session, you perform the following tasks:

1. Create a new application group window.

2. Create a new program item for an application group.

3. Select an icon for the new program item.

4. Delete a program item and application group.

5. Select a new color scheme for Windows.

6. Select a pattern and wallpaper for the Desktop.

7. Activate a screen saver utility for Windows.

8. Select and customize a printer.

9. Retrieve general and specific help for Windows.

Before proceeding, make sure the following are true:

1. You have turned on your computer system and loaded Windows 3.1.
2. The Program Manager window appears on the screen.
3. Your Advantage Diskette is inserted into drive A:. You will work with files on the diskette that have been created for you. (Note: The Advantage Diskette can be duplicated by copying all of the files from your instructor's Master Advantage Diskette.)

PROGRAM MANAGER

Windows enables you to organize your application programs into groups. Each application program and group is represented by an icon in Program Manager. When first installed, Windows automatically sets up several application groups for you, including Main and Accessories. The program items in these groups are listed alphabetically in Table 2.1.

Table 2.1	*Name*	*Icon*	*Description*
Applications provided with Windows	Calculator		General or scientific calculator
	Calendar		Daily diary and monthly planner program
	Cardfile		Small database program for storing phone numbers, addresses, or other information
	Character Map		Series of special symbols that you can insert into documents and applications
	Clipboard		Clipboard viewer for displaying data that appears in the memory buffer
	Clock		Analog or digital clock
	Control Panel		System program for setting screen and printer defaults and other configuration options
	File Manager		File and disk management program for copying files and formatting disks
	Media Player		Utility for playing MIDI audio files; a multimedia extension
	Minesweeper		Game

Table 2.1	*Name*	*Icon*	*Description*
Continued	MS-DOS Prompt		DOS command prompt
	Notepad		Small text editor for creating system initialization files (INI) and batch files (BAT)
	Object Packager		Program that creates objects for sharing and exchanging information between applications
	Paintbrush		Drawing program for creating, saving, and printing graphic pictures
	PIF Editor		Program for creating Program Information Files for DOS applications
	Print Manager		Program that manages jobs or documents sent to the printer
	Recorder		Macro recorder for saving keystrokes and mouse actions for later playback
	Solitaire		Klondike Solitaire game
	Sound Recorder		Program that records and plays back sounds; plays and edits audio WAV files
	Terminal		Communications program for connecting to other computers using a modem
	Write		Word processing program for creating, saving, and printing documents, such as letters

THE STARTUP GROUP

The StartUp group window enables you to launch applications each time you start Windows. Unlike the Main and Accessories groups, the StartUp group window is initially empty. To have Windows automatically load an application for you, you must place or copy an application's program icon into the StartUp group window. You copy an icon between group windows by holding down the Ctrl key as you drag the icon from one window to another.

Perform the following steps to have Windows automatically start the File Manager each time you load Windows.

1. Close all the open group windows in Program Manager.

2. Open the Main group window.

3. Open the StartUp group window.

4. CHOOSE: Window, Tile
    The two group windows are placed next to each other in the Program Manager application window. This type of window arrangement facilitates copying icons between groups.

5. PRESS: Ctrl and hold it down

6. Position the mouse pointer over the File Manager icon (⌷).

7. CLICK: left mouse button and hold it down
    DRAG: File Manager icon to the StartUp group window

8. Release the left mouse button and Ctrl key to complete the copy operation. Your screen should now appear similar to Figure 2.1.

Figure 2.1

Copying the File Manager program icon to the StartUp group window

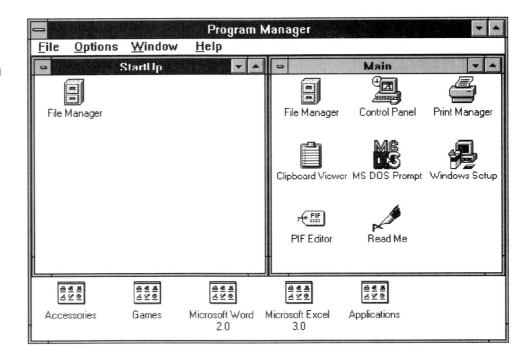

9. Having demonstrated copying a program icon to the StartUp group, you will now remove the File Manager icon:
PRESS: [Delete]
PRESS: [Enter] or CLICK: Yes

10. Close or minimize both group windows.

....

Quick Reference
The StartUp Group

- To automatically load an application each time you start Windows, place the application's program icon in the StartUp group.
- To copy an icon from one group window to another, press and hold down the [Ctrl] key and drag the icon between the windows.

....

CREATING GROUPS AND PROGRAM ITEMS

In addition to the application groups and programs provided by Windows, you can create and specify your own group windows and program items. Before creating a new group, you should minimize the open group windows in the Program Manager area. You use the File, New command to create application groups and program items.

Perform the following steps.

1. Ensure that the Advantage Diskette is placed into drive A: and that all the open group windows in Program Manager are closed.

2. To create a new application group called *Home Work*:
CHOOSE: File, New

3. SELECT: Program Group option button
(Note: When all group windows are minimized, the Program Group option is selected by default in the New Program Object dialog box.)

4. PRESS: [Enter] or CLICK: OK
The Program Group Properties dialog box appears for you to enter the name of the new application group.

5. In the Description text box, enter the name that will appear beneath the application group's icon:
TYPE: Home Work
PRESS: [Tab]

CAUTION: Do not press (Enter) until you are finished entering all the information into the dialog box. You use the mouse or press (Tab) and (Shift)+(Tab) to move through a dialog box, and then press (Enter) when you are finished entering information.

6. In the Group File text box, enter the name of the disk file for storing the information about this application group:
    TYPE: homework
    PRESS: (Enter) or CLICK: OK
    A new empty group window appears with the Title bar "Home Work."
    (Note: Keep the name of a group file to a maximum of eight letters with no spaces, following the DOS conventions for naming files.)

7. To create a program item in the new group window:
    CHOOSE: File, New

8. SELECT: Program Item
    PRESS: (Enter) or CLICK: OK
    The Program Item Properties dialog box is displayed (Figure 2.2).

Figure 2.2

The Program Item Properties dialog box

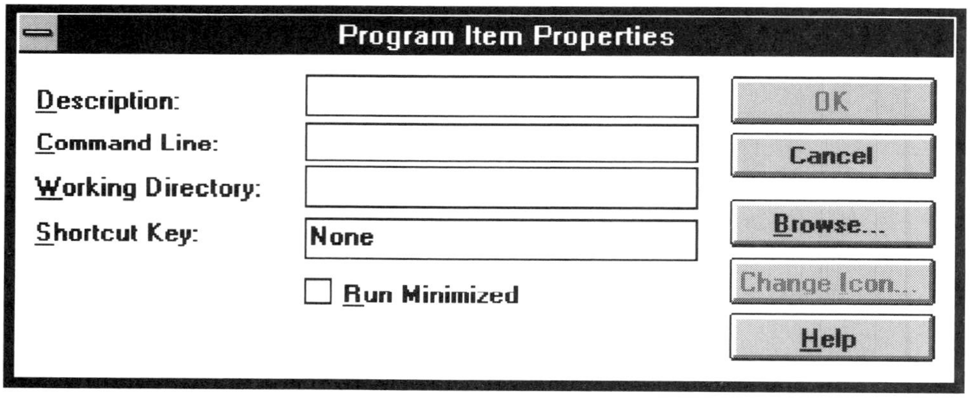

9. In the dialog box, you can specify a working directory for your application's data files and a shortcut key for moving quickly among running applications. If you leave the working directory text box blank, Windows assumes that the data files for your application are located in the same directory as the application program file. In this step, you create a program item icon for a DOS application called PHONES, located on the Advantage Diskette.

To enter the icon description in the Description text box:
TYPE: My Phone Book
PRESS: (Tab)

10. In the Command Line text box, enter the name of the application program file. For this example, the PHONES application file is called A:\PHONES.EXE. To enter the program filename:
TYPE: a:\phones.exe
PRESS: (Enter) or CLICK: OK

11. Because a removable path is specified (in other words, you can remove the Advantage Diskette from drive A:), you must confirm the operation:
CLICK: Yes
The MS-DOS program icon appears in the Home Work group window.

12. To start the PHONES application:
DOUBLE-CLICK: My Phone Book icon
The program loads from the diskette and, therefore, may take a few moments to appear.

13. To quit the PHONES application and return to Windows:
PRESS: (F10)

14. To modify the icon's title, you must select the program icon and then modify its properties:
CHOOSE: File, Properties
(Note: You can also press (Alt)+(Enter) to modify the properties of the currently selected program item.)

15. In the Description text box, enter a new name for the icon:
TYPE: Personal Phone Numbers
PRESS: (Enter) or CLICK: OK
CLICK: Yes to confirm the warning of a removable path

....

Quick Reference   1. To create a new application group or program item, choose File,
Creating a New   New and then select the appropriate option button.
Application Group   2. Press (Enter) or click on OK to proceed.
or Program Item   3. Type the desired icon title in the Description text box.
                         4. Type the filename in the Group File or Command Line text box.
                         5. Press (Enter) or click on OK.

....

CHANGING PROGRAM ICONS

In the last section you created a new program item for the PHONES application on the Advantage Diskette. When Windows does not recognize an application program, it provides a generic icon like the MS-DOS icon in the Home Work group window. You can easily change the icon assigned to a program item using the File, Properties command. Once the Program Item Properties dialog box is displayed, you choose the Change Icon command button to display the available icons.

To view additional icons, you can type a new file name in the File Name text box of the Change Icon dialog box. Some of the more popular icons appear in the MORICONS.DLL, PROGMAN.EXE, and SETUP.EXE files, located in the Windows directory. The PROGMAN.EXE and SETUP.EXE files contain Windows icons, whereas MORICONS.DLL contains over 100 icons for DOS application software programs.

Perform the following steps.

1. Ensure that the Home Work group window is open and that the Personal Phone Book icon is selected.

2. To edit the program item:
   PRESS: (Alt)+(Enter)
   Remember, (Alt)+(Enter) is the shortcut keystroke for accessing the File, Properties menu command.

3. To view the available icons:
   CLICK: Change Icon command button

4. Because no icons are associated with this file, Windows lets you select from the icons in the PROGMAN.EXE file:
   PRESS: (Enter) or CLICK: OK

5. To select a new icon from PROGMAN.EXE:
   CLICK: right arrow head on the horizontal scroll bar multiple times
   SELECT: the phone icon (☏)
   PRESS: (Enter) or CLICK: OK

6. To save the new properties for the program item:
   PRESS: (Enter) or CLICK: OK
   CLICK: Yes
   The new icon appears in the Home Work group window. Your screen should now appear similar to Figure 2.3.

Figure 2.3

The Home Work group window and Personal Phone Book program icon

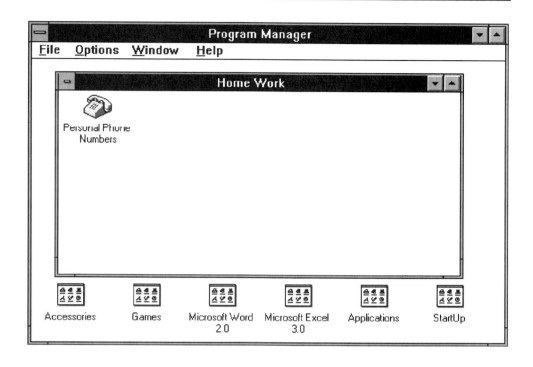

....

Quick Reference
Changing Program Item Icons

1. To change the icon for a program item, choose File, Properties and then select the Change Icon command button.
2. Select the desired icon from the horizontally scrolling list box.
3. Press (Enter) or click on OK to accept the new icon.
4. Press (Enter) or click on OK to accept the program properties.

....

DELETING GROUPS AND PROGRAM ITEMS

You remove a program item or application group window by choosing the File, Delete command from the menu or by pressing the (Delete) key. Before removing a program or group, you must first select the program icon, group window, or group icon. When asked for confirmation of the deletion, you respond by selecting Yes in the dialog box to permanently delete the program or group.

Perform the following steps.

1. CLICK: Personal Phone Numbers program item once

2. To remove the program item:
   PRESS: (Delete)

3. Confirm the deletion of the PHONES application:
   CLICK: Yes

4. To remove the Home Work application group window:
   CHOOSE: File, Delete
   CLICK: Yes

....

Quick Reference   1. Select the program item icon, group window, or group icon.
Removing a   2. To delete the selected object, choose File, Delete from the menu or
Program Item or   press (Delete).
Application Group   3. Press (Enter) or click on Yes to confirm the deletion.

....

CONTROL PANEL

With Control Panel, you can change the system defaults for your computer and printers. You not only can customize the appearance of the Desktop using color schemes, background patterns, and bitmap graphics (discussed in the Customizing the Desktop section), you can have Windows automatically blank the screen when it is not in use. To launch Control Panel, open the Main group window and then double-click on the Control Panel program icon. The Control Panel dialog box is similar to a special group window that contains several configuration programs. Most of these program item icons are listed in Table 2.2.

Table 2.2	*Name*	*Icon*	*Configuration Task*
Control Panel icons	Color		Select predefined color schemes or create your own color combinations for the screen
	Date/Time		Change the system date and time for the computer's internal clock
	Desktop		Specify a pattern or wallpaper graphic for the Desktop, and implement a screen saver utility

	Name	Icon	Configuration Task
Table 2.2 *Continued*	Drivers		Set up multimedia hardware components and software drivers
	Fonts		Define screen and printer fonts; add new fonts
	International		Change the keyboard layout, date and time display, and currency format
	Keyboard		Specify the keyboard speed and repeat rate
	Mouse		Set mouse tracking and double-clicking speeds, or swap the left and right mouse buttons
	Ports		Specify communication parameters for serial ports COM1, COM2, COM3, and COM4
	Printers		Select and configure the default printer, and specify whether to use Print Manager
	Sound		Assign sounds (WAV files) to Windows events
	386 Enhanced		If you are using a 386 or better computer in enhanced mode, this program lets you set the processing and virtual memory options

CHOOSING A COLOR SCHEME

Whether you use a color monitor, monochrome monitor, or liquid crystal display (LCD displays are common on laptop and notebook computers), you will appreciate the variety of color schemes available for Windows. While seemingly superficial, the ability to change colors is very important to notebook users who typically have VGA color capabilities with gray-scale LCD screens. To avoid eyestrain and losing the mouse pointer on these displays, you can pick and choose the best color combinations for contrast and shading.

Perform the following steps to change the Windows color scheme.

1. Open the Main group window.

2. Open the Control Panel dialog box:
    DOUBLE-CLICK: Control Panel icon

3. To change the color scheme, select the Color option:
    DOUBLE-CLICK: Color icon
    The Color dialog box appears.
    (Note: Keyboard users can select the Color command from the Settings
    menu option.)

4. To select a predefined color scheme, select the drop-down list box in
    the Color Schemes area:
    SELECT: Color Schemes drop-down list box
    You select the drop-down list box by clicking the down arrow that
    appears to the right of the box, or by pressing Alt + ↓.

5. To sample the various color schemes:
    PRESS: ↓ multiple times to scroll through the list
    Notice that the sample window below the drop-down list box displays
    the highlighted color selection.

6. SELECT: *any color scheme*

7. Save your selection and return to the Control Panel dialog box:
    PRESS: Enter or CLICK: OK

You can also select custom colors for individual screen elements, such as
borders, Title bars, and windows. To select custom colors, you choose the
Color Palette command button in the Color dialog box. The dialog box
expands to display a palette of colors (Figure 2.4). To apply a custom color
to a screen element, you click the screen element in the sample window and
then click the desired color from the palette. When finished selecting
colors, you can save your custom color scheme with the other Windows
schemes by choosing the Save Scheme command button.

Figure 2.4

Selecting custom colors from the Color dialog box

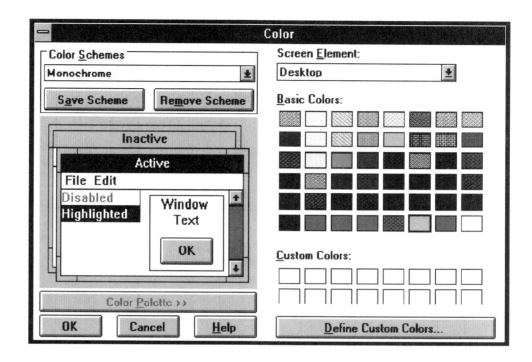

Quick Reference
*Choosing a Color
Scheme for
Windows*

1. Select the Color icon from the Control Panel dialog box, or choose the Settings, Color command.
2. Select a predefined color scheme from the drop-down list box.
3. Press (Enter) or click on OK.

CUSTOMIZING THE DESKTOP

You can customize the appearance of the Windows Desktop using patterns or **bitmap graphics** (images stored in disk files.) To display a pattern or bitmap graphic on the Desktop, you select the Desktop icon from the Control Panel dialog box. In the Desktop dialog box (Figure 2.5), select the name of the desired pattern or specify a file containing the bitmap graphic for wallpapering the Desktop. You are not limited to using the bitmap graphics provided by Windows for your wallpaper. In fact, many organizations display their company logo on the Windows Desktop. Although you can specify both a pattern and a wallpaper bitmap, wallpaper is always placed over a pattern.

Figure 2.5

The Desktop
dialog box

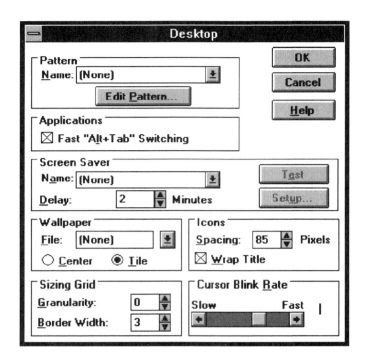

Perform the following steps.

1. Ensure that the Control Panel dialog box is displayed.

2. To apply a pattern to the Desktop, select the Desktop option:
    DOUBLE-CLICK: Desktop icon
    (Note: Keyboard users can select the Desktop command from the
    Settings menu option.)

3. To select a pattern, display the drop-down list box in the Patterns area:
    SELECT: Name drop-down list box
    You select the drop-down list box by clicking the down arrow that
    appears to the right of the box, or by pressing (Alt)+(↓).

4. To browse through the available patterns:
    CLICK: up and down arrows on the vertical scroll bar

5. CHOOSE: Critters pattern option
    To choose a pattern, click on the pattern name using the mouse or
    highlight the pattern and then press (Tab).

6. To view the pattern:
    PRESS: (Enter) or CLICK: OK

7. To better see the Desktop, minimize Program Manager. Do not, however, minimize the Control Panel dialog box.

8. To select a bitmap graphic for wallpapering the Desktop:
   DOUBLE-CLICK: Desktop icon in the Control Panel dialog box

9. To display the wallpaper bitmap graphic options:
   SELECT: File drop-down list box in the Wallpaper area

10. To browse the available wallpaper options:
    CLICK: up and down arrows on the vertical scroll bar

11. CHOOSE: WINLOGO.BMP from the list of wallpaper options

12. SELECT: Tile option button
    The Tile option reproduces the bitmap graphic until it fills the entire screen. The Center option places only one copy of the bitmap graphic in the center of the screen.

13. PRESS: [Enter] or CLICK: OK
    Notice that the previous pattern is covered by the wallpaper selection. You should see the Windows logo etched into the Desktop.

14. To remove the pattern and wallpaper, select the (None) option from each drop-down list box:
    DOUBLE-CLICK: Desktop icon in the Control Panel dialog box

15. Remove the pattern from the Name drop-down list box:
    SELECT: Name drop-down list box in the Patterns area
    SELECT: (None)

16. Remove the wallpaper from the File drop-down list box:
    SELECT: File drop-down list box in the Wallpaper area
    SELECT: (None)

17. PRESS: [Enter] or CLICK: OK

18. To restore the Program Manager window:
    DOUBLE-CLICK: Program Manager icon

Quick Reference   1. Select the Desktop icon from the Control Panel dialog box, or
Choosing a   choose the Settings, Desktop command.
Desktop Pattern or   2. Select the name of a background pattern or specify a file containing
Wallpaper   a bitmap graphic for wallpapering the Desktop.
                         3. Press (Enter) or click on OK.

USING A SCREEN SAVER

Windows provides a screen saver utility that protects the life of your monitor. When a static, unchanging screen image appears on the monitor for extended periods of time, the image may become etched into the monitor. A screen saver program automatically blanks your screen, or uses random moving objects, to avoid burning in a screen image on the monitor. You initiate the screen saver utility using the Desktop option.

Perform the following steps.

1. Ensure that the Control Panel dialog box is displayed.

2. To initiate a screen saver for Windows, select the Desktop option:
    DOUBLE-CLICK: Desktop icon

3. To select the type of screen saver:
    SELECT: Name drop-down list box in the Screen Saver area

4. To browse through the available screen savers:
    CLICK: up and down arrows on the vertical scroll bar

5. CHOOSE: Mystify option
    To choose a screen saver, click on the desired option using the mouse or highlight the option using the arrow keys and then press (Tab).

6. To test the screen saver:
    CLICK: Test command button
    The screen blanks and displays the selected screen saver option. You may need to click the mouse button again to return to the dialog box.

7. In the Delay box, you enter the number of minutes that should elapse without activity before displaying the screen saver. For this example, set the value to 10 minutes.

8. PRESS: (Enter) or CLICK: OK

Quick Reference
Choosing a Screen
Saver

1. Select the Desktop icon from the Control Panel dialog box, or choose the Settings, Desktop command.
2. Select a screen saver from the Name drop-down list box in the Screen Saver area.
3. Choose the Test button to view a sample of the screen saver. Once displayed, click the mouse button or press any key to return to the dialog box.
4. Specify the amount of time to wait before initiating the screen saver by entering a number in the Delay text box.
5. Press (Enter) or click on OK.

CHOOSING A PRINTER

The Control Panel enables you to add, modify, and remove **printer drivers**, the files that enable a software program to communicate with various types of printers. More importantly, you can specify and configure a default printer using the Printers option in the Control Panel dialog box. Once the Printers dialog box (Figure 2.6) is displayed, you select the desired printer and choose the Set as Default Printer command button. In the bottom left-hand corner, make sure the check box is selected to use the Print Manager. If Print Manager is not selected, you must wait for one document to finish printing before sending another document to the printer. To customize the settings for the default printer, select the Setup button to specify the paper source, number of copies to print, and **orientation** (in portrait orientation the page is printed upright similar to this page; in landscape it prints sideways).

Figure 2.6

Printers dialog
box

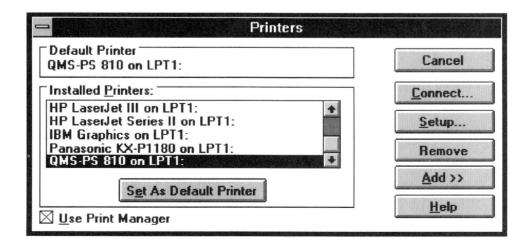

Perform the following steps to ensure that Print Manager is selected.

1. Ensure that the Control Panel dialog box is displayed.

2. To view the default printer settings, select the Printers option:
    DOUBLE-CLICK: Printers icon

3. Make sure that you are using the Print Manager. If there is not an X in
    the check box, do the following:
    SELECT: Use Print Manager check box
    Remember, a check box is selected when an X appears in the box.

4. To view the setup options for your default printer:
    CLICK: Setup command button

5. When you are finished viewing the setup options:
    PRESS: (Enter) or CLICK: OK

6. To exit the Printers dialog box:
    PRESS: (Enter) or CLICK: Close

7. To close the Control Panel dialog box:
    CHOOSE: Settings, Exit

Quick Reference
Choosing a
Default Printer

1. Select the Printers icon from the Control Panel dialog box, or
    choose the Settings, Printers command.
2. Select a printer from the list box.
3. Select the Set as Default Printer button.
4. Select the Setup button to customize the printer's default settings.
5. Press (Enter) or click on OK to save the Setup information.
6. Press (Enter) or click on Close to save the Printer information.

PRINT MANAGER

In a multitasking environment, application programs must share processing time, memory, and printer resources. Windows manages your system resources using programs like Print Manager, which coordinates and schedules documents that are sent to the printer from application programs. To handle the printing of multiple documents, Print Manager places documents temporarily in a print spooler or **queue** on the disk. When the printer has completed one print job, Print Manager takes the next print job from the queue and sends it to the printer. Because this spooling process occurs in the background, you can continue working in an application after sending a document to the printer.

If you select the Use Print Manager check box when specifying a default printer, Print Manager automatically loads each time you send a document to the printer. You can also manually load Print Manager by double-clicking the Print Manager icon in the Main group window. To load Print Manager each time you use Windows, copy the Print Manager icon into the StartUp group window.

With Print Manager, you monitor the active and inactive printers and the status of files that have been sent to the print queue. To display the time and date or file size of print jobs, choose the View, Time/Date Sent and View, Print File Size commands. A check mark appears beside these commands in the pull-down menu when they are active. Figure 2.7 shows the Print Manager window with three files sent to the QMS-PS810 printer attached to LPT1, while the other printers remain idle.

Figure 2.7

The Print
Manager window

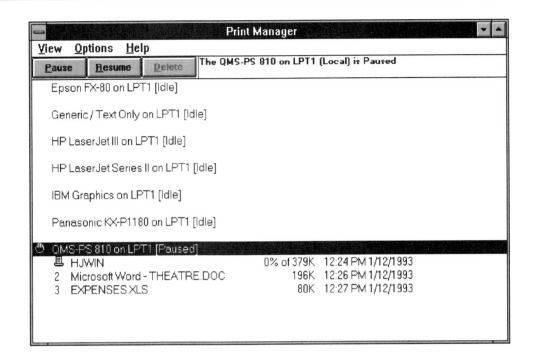

You can manipulate the print queue in Print Manager by reordering and
deleting files that appear in the list. For example, if you want to print a one-
page letter after sending several larger documents to the printer, you can
move the letter up in the print queue so that it is the next document in line
for the printer. However, you cannot move the first file in the queue. Using
a mouse, you move a file in the queue by dragging the file name. Using the
keyboard, you first highlight the file using the cursor-movement keys, and
then press Ctrl + ↑ to move a file up in the queue or Ctrl + ↓ to move
a file down in the queue. To delete a file, you select the file and then click
on the Delete button under the Menu bar or press Alt + d.

Besides changing the order of print jobs, you can affect the speed at which
documents are printed by changing their priority. Selecting Low Priority
from the Options menu, for example, gives your applications more
processing (CPU) time so that you can continuing working without a
severe degradation in speed. If you select High Priority, Windows
apportions more system resources to Print Manager than to your
application programs. The default setting for Print Manager is Medium
Priority.

GETTING HELP

Because you may not always remember the steps needed to perform an operation, Windows provides an extensive on-line Help facility. To retrieve context-sensitive help, press the `F1` key. **Context-sensitive** refers to Windows' ability to retrieve Help information for your current position in the program. The Help option on the Program Manager Menu bar allows you to access specific Help topics (Table 2.3).

Table 2.3	*Command*	*Description*
The Help menu	Contents	A topical index for getting help for Program Manager
	Search for Help on	A search facility for looking up Help information
	How to Use Help	Information on using the Help facility
	Windows Tutorial	Tutorial for using the mouse and manipulating windows
	About Program Manager	Displays version, mode, and memory information

Once a Help window is displayed, Windows provides several command buttons to control movement through the Help facility: Contents, Search, Back, History, and Glossary. Selecting the Contents button or Search button performs the same procedure as choosing their respective menu options. The Back button enables you to see the previous Help topic and the History button provides a scrollable list of all the topics you have viewed in the session. If you need to look up a word's definition, the Glossary button displays a glossary of terms in alphabetical order.

When you access a Help window (Figure 2.8), you may notice some words or phrases that have a solid or dotted underline. A solid underline denotes a **jump term** that you can select to jump to another Help topic for additional information. To move to jump terms or definitions in a Help window, you use the mouse or press `Tab` and `Shift`+`Tab`. A word or phrase that has a dotted underline provides a definition box when selected.

Figure 2.8

The Help facility

Perform the following steps to access the Help facility using the Menu bar.

1. To display a directory of the Help facility contents:
   CHOOSE: Help, Contents from the menu

2. To move the Selection cursor in the Help window:
   PRESS: [Tab] several times to move down through the choices, and then [Shift]+[Tab] to move back up

3. To retrieve help on quitting Windows, highlight the appropriate option:
   PRESS: [Tab] or [Shift]+[Tab] until the Quit Windows topic is highlighted under the How To... section

4. PRESS: [Enter]

5. After reading the Help information, close the window:
   CHOOSE: File, Exit
   (Note: You can also double-click the Control menu for the Program Manager Help window.)

6. To get help on the Options, Save Settings on Exit command, you can highlight the option in the pull-down menu and then press [F1]:
   PRESS: [Alt]+o
   PRESS: [↓] twice until Save Settings on Exit is highlighted
   PRESS: [F1]
   A Help window for the command is displayed.

7. After reading the Help information, close the window:
   DOUBLE-CLICK: Control menu for the Help window

8. To display memory status and copyright information:
   CHOOSE: Help, About Program Manager

9. After reading the information:
   PRESS: [Enter] or CLICK: OK

....

Quick Reference   • Press [F1] to display context-sensitive help.
Using Help   • Highlight an option on a pull-down menu and press [F1] to display
                        context-sensitive help for a menu command.
                      • Choose Help, Contents to display a list of Help topics.
                      • Choose Help, About to display memory and copyright information.
                      • Choose File, Exit or double-click the Control menu on the Program
                        Manager Help window to close a Help window.

....

SUMMARY

Building on the skills you learned in Session 1, this session explored more features of the Program Manager. You not only created an application program group but added a program item, changed a program item's icon, and learned how to delete program icons and groups. This session also introduced the Control Panel for setting up and customizing Windows. You examined the Color option for changing the screen colors, the Desktop option for choosing Desktop patterns and wallpaper, and the Printers option for specifying and configuring printers. A brief section on Print Manager introduced several commands and techniques that enhance printing in Windows applications. The final topic in the session explored the Windows Help facility, where you retrieved help on general and specific topics for Program Manager.

Many of the commands and procedures introduced in this session appear in the Command Summary (Table 2.4).

	Command	Description
Table 2.4 Command Summary	*Command*	*Description*
	File, New	Create a new program group or program item
	File, Properties	Modify an item's properties, such as its name and icon
	File, Delete	Delete a program item or program group
	View, Time/Date Sent	In Print Manager, display the time and date that each file was sent to the print queue
	View, Print File Size	In Print Manager, display the size of each file in the print queue
	Options, Low Priority	Give applications more CPU time than Print Manager
	Options, Medium Priority	Give applications and Print Manager equal CPU time
	Options, High Priority	Give applications less CPU time than Print Manager
	Help, *command*	Retrieve information from the Windows Help facility

KEY TERMS

bitmap graphics   A graphic image or picture that is stored in a disk file as a series or pattern of dots.

context-sensitive   Refers to Windows' ability to retrieve help for your current position in the program.

jump term   In the Windows Help facility, click on a jump term to move to another Help topic. Jump terms are underlined with a solid line.

orientation   Describes how a page is printed. Letter-size paper with a portrait orientation measures 8.5" wide by 11" high. Letter-size paper with a landscape orientation measures 11" wide by 8.5" high.

printer drivers   Files stored on a disk containing instructions that enable a software program to communicate with a printer.

queue   An area of Print Manager that uses memory and the disk to line up and prioritize documents waiting for the printer.

EXERCISES

SHORT ANSWER

1. What is the purpose of the StartUp program group?
2. How do you copy a program icon from one group window to another?
3. What two options appear when you choose File, New from the Program Manager menu?
4. Explain the purpose of the Working Directory text box in the Program Item Properties dialog box.
5. What information does Windows insert into the Working Directory text box if you leave it blank?
6. Name three files from which you can choose icons for program items.
7. What is meant by the term *wallpaper your Desktop*?
8. What must you do to ensure that the Print Manager program handles the printing of your documents?
9. How do you change the order of documents once they appear in the Print Manager queue?
10. Explain how *jump terms* work in the Windows Help facility.

HANDS-ON

(Note: In the following exercises, you perform Windows commands using files located on the Advantage Diskette.)

1. This exercise practices creating application program groups and program items. To choose a new program item icon, you use the MORICONS.DLL file from the Windows directory.
   a. Ensure that the Advantage Diskette is placed into drive A:.
   b. Start your computer and load DOS.
   c. Load Microsoft Windows 3.1 and wait for the Program Manager application window to appear.
   d. Close all open group windows.

e. To create a new group window for your business documents:
    CHOOSE: File, New
    SELECT: Program Group option
    PRESS: (Enter) or CLICK: OK

f. In the Description text box, enter the name for the new group:
    TYPE: Business Folder
    PRESS: (Tab)

g. In the Group File text box, enter the name of the disk storage file:
    TYPE: business
    PRESS: (Enter)
    A new group window appears with the words "Business Folder" in the Title bar.

h. To reposition the window:
    CHOOSE: Window, Cascade

i. To add a program item to the new group window:
    CHOOSE: File, New
    SELECT: Program Item option
    PRESS: (Enter) or CLICK: OK

j. In the Program Item Properties dialog box, you enter the program file name and any other parameters for the new program item. For this exercise, you will create a program item that uses the Windows Notepad program to read a text file on the Advantage Diskette. To begin, enter the name for the program item in the Description box:
    TYPE: Example Business Document
    PRESS: (Tab)

k. In the Command Line dialog box, you enter the program filename and the document filename, separated by a space:
    TYPE: notepad.exe a:\example.txt
    PRESS: (Enter)
    A program icon, modeled after the Notepad application icon, appears in the group window. (Note: Do not worry if you are confused by this step. This exercise merely demonstrates what you can do with program items. You are not expected to know the names of the Windows programs, such as NOTEPAD.EXE.) Your screen should, however, appear similar to Figure 2.9 before continuing.

Figure 2.9

Creating a
program item icon
in the Business
Folder's group
window

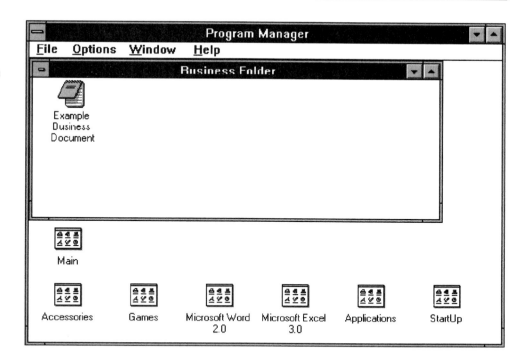

l. To see how this program item works:
    DOUBLE-CLICK: Example Business Document icon
    After a few moments, the Notepad program opens the
    EXAMPLE.TXT file that appears on the Advantage Diskette.
m. CHOOSE: File, Exit from the Notepad window
n. To change the program item's icon:
    CHOOSE: File, Properties
    CLICK: Change Icon
    Only one icon appears in the horizontal scroll area.
o. To retrieve other icons:
    TYPE: moricons.dll into the File Name text box
    PRESS: (Enter)
    The horizontal scroll area should fill with new icons.
p. Browse the icons using the mouse or cursor-movement keys.
q. SELECT: ▨ icon
r. PRESS: (Enter) or CLICK: OK
s. PRESS: (Enter) or CLICK: OK
    The new icon appears in the group window.

t. To clean house in the Program Manager window, delete the Example Business Document program icon and the Business Folder group window:
    PRESS: (Delete)
    CLICK: Yes to confirm the deletion of the program item
    PRESS: (Delete)
    CLICK: Yes to confirm the deletion of the group window

2. This exercise practices customizing the Desktop using the pattern and wallpaper options.
    a. Ensure that the Advantage Diskette is placed into drive A:.
    b. Ensure that the Main group window is the only open window in Program Manager.
    c. Open the Control Panel dialog box:
        DOUBLE-CLICK: Control Panel icon
    d. To customize the Desktop:
        DOUBLE-CLICK: Desktop option
    e. To specify a background pattern for the Desktop, select the Name drop-down list box in the Pattern area:
        SELECT: Name drop-down list box
    f. CHOOSE: Quilt option
    g. PRESS: (Enter) or CLICK: OK
        You should see the pattern change on the background screen. If the pattern does not appear on the Desktop, make sure that the Wallpaper option in the Desktop dialog box is (None).
    h. Minimize the Program Manager window.
    i. To display a bitmap graphic on the Desktop:
        DOUBLE-CLICK: Desktop option
    j. For patterns, specify (None) in the Name drop-down list box.
    k. To specify a bitmap graphic for the Desktop, select the File drop-down list box in the Wallpaper area:
        SELECT: File drop-down list box
    l. CHOOSE: CASTLE.BMP option
    m. PRESS: (Enter) or CLICK: OK
    n. Practice selecting other bitmap graphics from the File drop-down list box. Before proceeding to the next exercise, select (None) as the file name in the Wallpaper area.

3. In this exercise, you navigate the Help facility to retrieve information on several topics.
    a. Browse the contents of the Microsoft Windows Help facility. Start by choosing the Help, Contents command from the Program Manager application window.

b. Under the How To section in the Help window:
   CLICK: Organize Applications and Documents option
c. CLICK: Changing Properties option
d. Notice that there are two words in the first sentence that have dotted underlines. To view the definition for *program item*, position the hand-shaped mouse pointer over the words and then do the following:
   CLICK: left mouse button once
e. After reading the definition, remove the definition box:
   CLICK: definition box
f. To view the definition for *group*:
   PRESS: [Tab] until the word is highlighted
   PRESS: [Enter]
g. After reading the definition, remove the definition box:
   PRESS: [Enter]
h. To return to the contents area:
   CLICK: Contents button
i. Under the How To section:
   CLICK: Change an Icon
j. To view a list of all the Help topics that you have selected:
   CLICK: History button
   Your screen should now appear similar to Figure 2.10.

Figure 2.10

History dialog box displayed with a Help Window

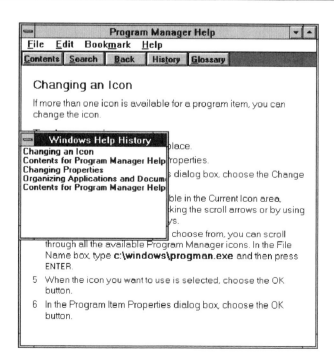

k. To close the Windows Help History dialog box:
   DOUBLE-CLICK: Control menu for the History dialog box

l. Return to the contents area.

m. To display the Windows Help Glossary:
   CLICK: Glossary button

n. Look up the word *wallpaper* and write down the exact definition that appears in the glossary.

o. Close the Glossary dialog box.

p. Close the Help facility.

WINDOWS 3.1: MANAGING YOUR WORK

If you have ever worked with a poorly organized hard disk, you know that good directory management can make your life much easier. For the same reasons you arrange folders in a filing cabinet or organize your desk, you use directories to manage your work on disks. With the Windows File Manager, you can perform routine disk, directory, and file management tasks, such as formatting diskettes, creating directories, copying files, or deleting an entire disk's contents.

PREVIEW

When you have completed this session, you will be able to:

Explain the importance of a directory structure.

•

Load File Manager.

•

Customize and work with directory windows.

•

Copy, move, rename, and delete files.

•

Create a directory structure.

•

Copy files among subdirectories.

•

Rename and remove directories.

SESSION OUTLINE

Why Is This Session Important?
What Is File Management?
What Is Disk Management?
File- and Disk-Naming Conventions
File Manager
Using File Manager
     The Guided Tour
     Customizing the Directory Window
     Selecting Drives
     Selecting Files
Managing Files
     Customizing the Directory Contents Pane
     Working with Multiple Directory Windows
     Copying and Moving Files
     Renaming Files
     Deleting Files
Managing Disks and Directories
     Creating a Directory
     Selecting a Directory
     Copying and Moving Files to Subdirectories
     Removing a Directory
     Renaming a Directory
     Preparing New Disks
     Naming a Disk
Summary
     Command Summary
Key Terms
Exercises
     Short Answer
     Hands-On

WHY IS THIS SESSION IMPORTANT?

This session introduces the procedures for managing your files and disks in Windows. File management involves copying, moving, renaming, and deleting individual files and groups of files. Directory or disk management focuses on creating and working with directory structures on hard disks and floppy diskettes, rather than the individual files on those disks. In this session, you perform the following file and disk management tasks using the Windows File Manager:

1. Copy files from one disk to another disk.

2. Move files from one disk to another disk.

3. Change the name of a file.

4. Delete files to free up space on a disk.

5. Create a directory structure.

6. Copy files among directories.

7. Rename directories.

8. Remove directories.

9. Name a disk using a volume label.

Before proceeding, make sure the following are true:

1. You have turned on your computer system and loaded Windows 3.1.
2. The Program Manager window appears on the screen.
3. Your Advantage Diskette is inserted into drive A:. You will work with files on the diskette that have been created for you. (Note: The Advantage Diskette can be duplicated by copying all of the files from your instructor's Master Advantage Diskette.)

WHAT IS FILE MANAGEMENT?

File management is the process of managing the work that you create and store on hard disks and floppy diskettes. Each document that you write or spreadsheet that you construct is stored in a disk file, similar to a file folder in a manual filing system. Managing your work involves copying, renaming, and deleting files. Table 3.1 shows the similarities between a manual and a computerized file management system.

	Manual System	*Computerized System*
Table 3.1 File management: comparison	Place a document in a filing cabinet for permanent storage	Save a document in a disk file for permanent storage on the hard disk or a floppy diskette
	Use a photocopier to duplicate an important document	Copy or back up an important disk file to another disk storage location
	Throw away old documents to free up room in the filing cabinet	Delete old files from the hard disk or a floppy diskette to free up disk space
	File a document under a new name	Rename a disk file

There are three categories of files that appear on hard disks and floppy diskettes: program files, document files, and data files. **Program files** consist of computer instructions for performing a certain task or for running an application software program. **Document files** contain work that you create using an application program recognized by Windows. For example, Windows knows that a disk file with the letters WRI for its extension was created using the Windows Write word processing program. Those documents for which Windows does not recognize the files' extensions are called **data files**. The file management principles discussed in this session apply equally to program, document, and data files.

What Is Disk Management?

Disk management is the process of managing the storage areas in your computer. Because one hard disk can store data that would normally fill several large filing cabinets, you must learn how to organize your files and maintain your disks. On a new disk, there is only one area for storing files: the **root directory**. Although the capacity of a root directory is limited to storing 512 files, you can easily create additional directories on the hard disk called **subdirectories**.

Think of the root directory as the top of a filing cabinet and each subdirectory as a drawer or folder in the cabinet. Obviously, you could not continually place documents on top of a cabinet without the files reaching the ceiling. One solution would be move the files from the top of the filing cabinet into the cabinet drawers. On a computer disk, the "ceiling" is the maximum number of files allowed in the root directory. Instead of moving file folders into cabinet drawers, you move files from the root directory to subdirectories on the hard disk. A hard disk's capacity for subdirectories is vast compared to a filing cabinet's capacity for folders. You can also create subdirectories within subdirectories. The organization of subdirectories on a hard disk is called a **directory structure** or **directory tree**.

In addition to creating directory structures, disk management involves preparing new disks for storing data and labeling disks. Table 3.2 compares a manual with a computerized storage system.

Table 3.2	*Manual System*	*Computerized System*
Directory and disk management: comparison	Label folders and drawers in a filing cabinet for holding related information	Create subdirectories for holding related disk files
	Prepare a new filing cabinet	Format or initialize a new disk
	Set aside and name a filing cabinet for a special purpose	Create a label or name for a hard disk or a floppy diskette

FILE- AND DISK-NAMING CONVENTIONS

Before you can perform file and disk management operations, you need to know the following DOS rules for naming files and disk drives:

1. A complete filename consists of a file name and an extension, separated by a period (for example, FILENAME.EXT). Every disk file must have a name; however, the extension is optional. The name of a file reflects its content, while the extension commonly indicates the application software program used to create the file. For example, the Windows Write program attaches an extension of WRI to all documents that you create in the application.

2. A file name can contain one to eight characters, with no spaces.

3. An **extension** can contain up to three characters, with no spaces.

4. Although you can use some special symbols in a file name, such as the ampersand (&) or underscore (_), try to use only letters and numbers. You must avoid symbols that DOS reserves (for example, *, ?, |, <, >).

Filename extensions allow you to categorize your work. Some application software programs automatically attach an extension to a file when it is saved to the disk—you only type the file name without the extension. By looking at extensions, you can immediately tell what data files were created by which programs. Other application programs, such as word processing programs, allow you to enter your own extensions for classifying files.

There are several possible disk drive configurations for microcomputers, and knowing how to reference each storage area is crucial to working with DOS and Windows. The first diskette drive is always referred to as drive A:. If your computer has two diskette drives, drive A: is usually positioned to the left or above the second diskette drive, called drive B:. If your computer has a hard disk drive, it is referred to as drive C:. The drive letter is always followed by a colon (:) to represent a drive designation.

FILE MANAGER

File Manager enables you to perform file and disk management activities using Menu bar commands, keyboard shortcuts, and mouse movements. Accessed from the Main group window in Program Manager, File Manager provides a graphical view of a disk's directory structure and files.

File Manager offers two important features: drag and drop file management and file association. **Drag and drop** file management lets you copy, move, and print disk files by dragging file icons using a mouse. **File association** enables you to select a document file and have Windows automatically load the application that was used to create the file. Before being associated with an application program, a document file is called a data file. Drag and drop file management, described later in this session, and file association, described in Session 5, help increase your productivity and reduce the time you spend managing your work.

With File Manager you are able to perform most DOS management tasks using Windows' menu-driven visual interface. Where once you entered long cryptic DOS commands at the C:\> prompt to manage your work, you now point, click, and drag icons using a mouse. The remainder of this session uses File Manager to demonstrate the more common file and disk management procedures.

USING FILE MANAGER

You load File Manager by selecting the File Manager icon from the Main group of the Program Manager window. Using a mouse, open the Main group window and then double-click on the File Manager icon. Using the keyboard, choose the Main group from the <u>W</u>indow option on the Menu bar. Once the Main group is open, select the File Manager icon using the cursor-movement keys and then press (**Enter**).

Perform the following steps to load File Manager.

1. Ensure that the Program Manager window is displayed.

2. Open the Main group window.

3.   DOUBLE-CLICK: File Manager icon (⊟)
     Your screen should now appear similar to Figure 3.1. (<u>Note</u>: The files
     and directories on your computer will differ from those in Figure 3.1.)

Figure 3.1

File Manager
application
window

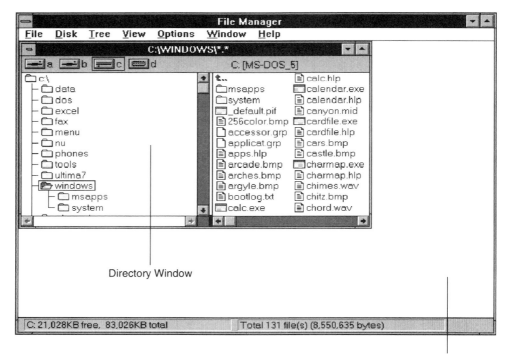

Directory Window

Application Window

Quick Reference   1.   Open the Main group window in the Program Manager window.
Loading File   2.   Double-click the File Manager icon.
Manager

THE GUIDED TOUR

When you first load File Manager, a single **directory window** appears in
the application window (Figure 3.1). Directory windows display the
directory structure and contents of disk drives. To facilitate managing files
on various drives, you can open several directory windows simultaneously
in the File Manager application window. You can also move, size, and
arrange directory windows within File Manager to best suit your needs and
available work space.

At the top of the application window, File Manager provides a menu for choosing file and disk management commands. The Status bar, located at the bottom of the application window, displays information for the selected disk drive and the highlighted directory. The left side of the Status bar shows the available space and total capacity of the selected drive. The right side of the Status bar shows the number of files in the selected directory, along with their accumulated size.

The directory window is divided into two panes by a vertical line called the **Split bar**. The left pane contains a graphical depiction of the directory tree for the selected disk drive. The right pane displays the contents of the highlighted folder in the directory tree. As explained later in this session, you can move the Split bar using the keyboard or a mouse to increase or decrease the viewing area in either pane. Other important components of a directory window are shown in Figure 3.2, including the drive icons, directory path, directory icons, file icons, scroll bars, and **Selection cursor**.

Figure 3.2

Components of a directory window

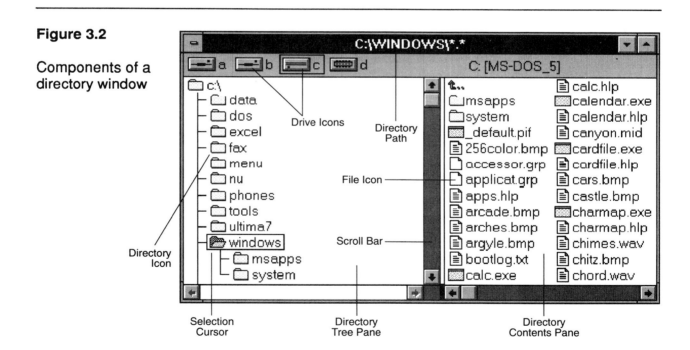

To work efficiently with a directory window, you must know how to manipulate its icons. Table 3.3 describes the components in a directory window.

Table 3.3	*Component*	*Description*
Explanation of the components in a directory window	Directory path	The directory window Title bar contains the **file specification**, including the current directory path. Because the asterisk **wildcard character** stands for any group of characters, the *.* specification displays all files in the selected directory.
	Drive icons (▭c)	Located beneath the directory window Title bar. You select a drive icon to display its directory tree and contents.
	Volume label	The volume label for the selected disk drive appears to the right of the drive icons area.
	Directory icons (□)	A folder icon represents a directory or subdirectory.
	Program file icon (□)	A program file icon represents a program or batch file. A program file typically has one of the following extensions: COM, EXE, PIF, or BAT.
	Document file icon (▤)	A document file icon represents a data file that is associated with an application.
	Data file icon (□)	A data file icon represents a file that is not associated with an application.
	Up icon (🗁..)	In the directory contents pane, you select the Up icon to move to the previous level or directory in the directory tree pane.
	Scroll bars	Scroll bars in the directory window facilitate moving through the directory tree pane and directory contents pane using a mouse.
	Selection cursor	You use the Selection cursor to select a drive icon, directory folder icon, or file icon.

CUSTOMIZING THE DIRECTORY WINDOW

A directory window initially displays the directory tree pane and the directory contents pane. You can also display a single pane in the directory window using the Yiew menu option. To view the directory tree pane only, choose the Tree Only option from the Yiew pull-down menu. To view the directory contents pane only, choose the Directory Only option. By default, the Tree and Directory option is selected in the Yiew pull-down menu.

Rather than splitting the directory window equally, you can adjust the area apportioned to each pane using the Split bar. With a mouse, you drag the Split bar to increase and decrease the share of the directory window occupied by each pane. With the keyboard, you select the Yiew, Split command and then press the ⬅ and ➡ keys.

Perform the following steps to customize your directory window.

1. To display the directory tree only in the directory window:
   CHOOSE: Yiew, Tree Only
   Notice that the active option in the pull-down menu has a check mark beside the command.

2. To display the directory contents only in the directory window:
   CHOOSE: Yiew, Directory Only

3. To display both the directory tree pane and directory contents pane:
   CHOOSE: Yiew, Tree and Directory

4. To adjust the area occupied by each pane:
   CHOOSE: Yiew, Split

5. You position the Split bar by pressing the cursor-movement keys or moving the mouse pointer. To maximize the directory contents area with the keyboard, position the Split bar just right of the directory tree:
   PRESS: ⬅ several times

6. To lock the new position for the Split bar:
   PRESS: (Enter)

7. To return the Split bar to an equal position between the panes:
   CHOOSE: Yiew, Tree and Directory

Quick Reference
Customizing the
Display of the
Directory Window
- To view the directory tree pane only, choose View, Tree Only.
- To view the contents pane only, choose View, Directory Only.
- To view both panes, choose View, Tree and Directory.
- To change the area occupied by each pane, choose View, Split and move the Split bar using the mouse or cursor-movement keys.

SELECTING DRIVES

To display the directory tree and files for a disk drive, you select the drive using the keyboard or a mouse. Using the keyboard, choose Disk, Select Drive from the menu to display a dialog box with the available disk drives. Once the dialog box appears, highlight the desired drive in the list box and then press (Enter) or click OK.

A shortcut method for selecting a drive using the keyboard is to press and hold down the (Ctrl) key and then tap the desired drive letter. For example, (Ctrl)+c selects drive C: and (Ctrl)+a selects drive A:. Using a mouse, you click once on the desired drive icon.

Perform the following steps.

1. Ensure that the Advantage Diskette is placed into drive A:.

2. To view the directory tree and files on drive A:, do the following:
   PRESS: (Ctrl)+a

3. To view the directory tree and files on drive C:, do the following:
   CLICK: drive C: icon (▭c) once

4. To reselect drive A: using the Select Drive command:
   CHOOSE: Disk, Select Drive
   SELECT: A: from the list box
   PRESS: (Enter) or CLICK: OK

Quick Reference
Selecting a Disk
Drive
- Using the Menu bar, choose the Disk, Select Drive command, highlight the desired drive in the list box, and then press (Enter).
- Using the keyboard, press and hold down the (Ctrl) key and then tap the desired drive letter.
- Using a mouse, click once on the desired drive icon.

SELECTING FILES

File Manager is based on a "Select" and then "Do" approach, where you highlight directories and files and then execute commands from the menu. When you select a directory in the directory tree pane, the subdirectories and files in that directory are displayed in the directory contents pane. To select files using the keyboard, you must first move to the directory contents pane. Use (Tab) and (Shift)+(Tab) to cycle between the drive icons area, the directory tree pane, and the directory contents pane.

SELECTING FILES USING THE KEYBOARD   Use the following methods to select files after moving to the directory contents pane:

1. *Selecting a single file.*
   To select a single file, highlight the file with the Selection cursor using the cursor-movement keys. Press (Home) to move to the first item and press (End) to move to the last item in the pane. A file is selected when it appears highlighted in reverse video.

2. *Selecting a small group of contiguous files.*
   To select a small group of contiguous files, position the Selection cursor on the first file, hold down the (Shift) key, and press (↓) to highlight each additional file. When finished, release the (Shift) key.

3. *Selecting a large group of contiguous files.*
   To select a large group of contiguous files, position the Selection cursor on the first file and then press (Shift)+(F8). (Note: On most displays, the Selection cursor begins to blink.) Position the highlight bar on the last file in the group and press (Shift)+Space Bar. All the files between the first and last file are selected. Press (Shift)+(F8) again to complete the file selection.

4. *Selecting a group of noncontiguous files.*
   To select a group of noncontiguous files, position the Selection cursor on the first file and then press (Shift)+(F8). Position the Selection cursor on each additional file and press the Space Bar to select. Once all the files are selected, press (Shift)+(F8) a second time.

5. *Selecting all of the files.*
   To select all of the files in the directory contents pane, press and hold down (Ctrl) and then press the forward slash (/). You may also choose the File, Select Files command from the menu. In the dialog box, choose the Select command button to highlight all the files and then choose Close.

6. *Removing the selection.*
   To remove the selection of files in the directory contents pane, press and hold down `Ctrl` and then press the backslash (\). The highlight is removed from all previously selected files. You may also choose the File, Select Files command from the menu. In the dialog box, choose the Deselect command button and then choose Close.

SELECTING FILES USING A MOUSE   Use the following methods to select files after moving to the directory contents pane:

1. *Selecting a single file.*
   To select a single file in the directory contents pane, position the mouse pointer over the file and click the left mouse button once.

2. *Selecting a group of contiguous files.*
   To select a group of contiguous files, position the mouse pointer over the first file and click the left mouse button once to select the file. Then position the mouse pointer over the last file in the group, hold down the `Shift` key, and click once. All the files between the first and last file are selected. Once the files are highlighted, release the `Shift` key.

3. *Selecting a group of noncontiguous files.*
   To select a group of noncontiguous files, position the mouse pointer over the first file and click the left mouse button once to select the file. Position the mouse pointer on each additional file, hold down the `Ctrl` key, and click once to select. Repeat this `Ctrl`+click sequence until all the desired files are selected, and then release the `Ctrl` key.

Perform the following steps to practice selecting files using the keyboard and mouse.

1. To display files for drive A: sorted by file name:
   PRESS: `Ctrl`+a
   CHOOSE: View, Sort by Name from the Menu bar
   The directory window Title bar displays the A:*.* file specification.

2. Select the directory contents pane by pressing `Tab` until the Selection cursor appears in the area.

3. To move to the end of the file list:
   PRESS: `End`

4. To move to the beginning of the list:
   PRESS: `Home`

5. To select the first five files in the list using the keyboard:
   PRESS: [Shift] and hold it down
   PRESS: [↓] four times

6. Release the [Shift] key.

7. To select the first five files in the list using a mouse:
   PRESS: [Home] to remove the previous selection
   PRESS: [Shift] and hold it down
   CLICK: the fifth file in the list
   Notice that the [Home] key moved the Selection cursor to the top of the list and automatically highlighted the first file.

8. Release the [Shift] key.

9. To select three noncontiguous files using the keyboard:
   PRESS: [Home] to remove the previous selection
   PRESS: [Shift]+[F8]

10. PRESS: [↓] three times
    PRESS: Space Bar to select the file
    Notice that the first file in the list remains highlighted.

11. PRESS: [↓] twice
    PRESS: Space Bar to select the file
    PRESS: [Shift]+[F8]
    Your screen should now appear similar to Figure 3.3.

Figure 3.3

Selecting multiple
files using the
keyboard

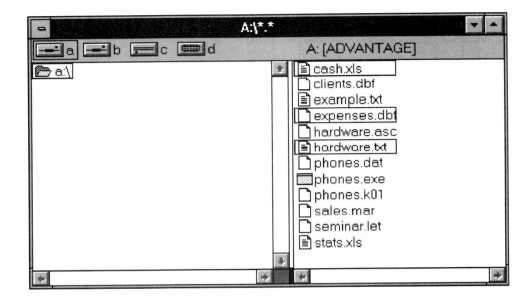

12. PRESS: [Home] to remove the previous selection

13. To select five noncontiguous files using a mouse:
    CLICK: *on a single file*

14. PRESS: [Ctrl] and hold it down
    CLICK: *on four additional files*

15. To remove the highlighting, release the [Ctrl] key and then click on any
    file in the directory contents pane.

Quick Reference   1. Position the Selection cursor on the first file to select.
Selecting Files   2. PRESS: [Shift]+[F8]
Using the   3. Position the Selection cursor on each additional file to include in the
Keyboard   selection and press the Space Bar to select.
                        4. PRESS: [Shift]+[F8]

Quick Reference
Selecting Files
Using a Mouse

1. Click the mouse pointer on the first file to select.
2. Press and hold down the [Ctrl] key.
3. Click the mouse pointer on each additional file to include in the selection.
4. Release the [Ctrl] key.

MANAGING FILES

Managing files involves displaying, organizing, selecting, copying, moving, renaming, and deleting files. The previous section discussed selecting files in the directory contents pane. In addition to customizing the display of files, this section introduces several methods for issuing commands. Although most file management commands are available from the File pull-down menu, you can also use keyboard shortcuts and drag and drop mouse techniques.

CUSTOMIZING THE DIRECTORY CONTENTS PANE

Working with the directory contents pane in its default view is sufficient for many users. However, it is often necessary to see additional file information, such as the size of a file and when it was last modified. Using the View menu option, you customize and sort the file information displayed in the directory contents pane.

VIEWING FILE DETAILS   To view the file details for files in the directory contents pane, choose the View, All File Details command from the menu. If you want to see the date that a file was last modified along with the name of a file, choose View, Partial Details and select the appropriate dialog box options. To show the maximum number of files in the directory window, use the View, Name option to display the file name and extension only.

Perform the following steps.

1. Ensure that the directory window displays the A:*.* file specification.

2. To view all the file details in the directory contents pane:
   CHOOSE: View, All File Details

3. Using a mouse, expand the directory window by dragging its sizing corner to the right. If you cannot see all the file detail information, reduce the area occupied by the directory tree pane using the Split bar. Your screen should appear similar to Figure 3.4.

Figure 3.4

Viewing all file details

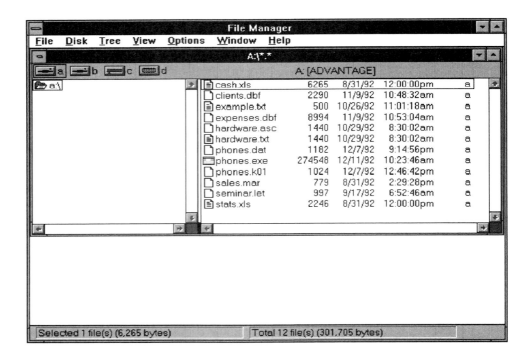

4. To view the name, size, and date information for files:
   CHOOSE: View, Partial Details
   SELECT: Size check box
   SELECT: Last Modification Date check box
   Remember that an item is selected when an X appears in the check box.

5. Remove the X from the Last Modification Time and File Attributes check boxes.

6. PRESS: (Enter) or CLICK: OK

Quick Reference
Viewing File Details
in the Directory
Contents Pane

- To view filenames only, choose View, Name from the menu.
- To view all file details, choose View, All File Details from the menu.
- To select the file details to display, choose View, Partial Details from the menu.

SORTING FILES   To sort the files in the directory contents pane, choose one of the View, Sort By commands: Sort by Name, Sort by Type, Sort by Size, or Sort by Date. Most of these sort options are self-explanatory. The active sort order has a check mark appearing beside the command in the View pull-down menu.

Perform the following steps.

1. To sort files according to size in the directory contents window:
    CHOOSE: View, Sort by Size

2. To sort files according to their filename extensions:
    CHOOSE: View, Sort by Type

3. To sort files according to name (the default):
    CHOOSE: View, Sort by Name

4. To view only the names of files in the directory contents pane:
    CHOOSE: View, Name

Quick Reference
Sorting Files in the
Directory Contents
Pane

- To sort files by filename, choose View, Sort by Name.
- To sort files by extension, choose View, Sort by Type.
- To sort files by size, choose View, Sort by Size.
- To sort files by date of last modification, choose View, Sort by Date.

LIMITING THE DISPLAY OF FILES   When you first load File Manager, the file specification is *.* and is preceded with the current drive letter and directory (for example, A:\ or C:\WINDOWS). The *.* specification tells File Manager to display all files in the current directory. To limit the display of files in the directory contents pane, choose the View, By File Type command. In the dialog box, you enter the desired file specification and choose individual check boxes for including subdirectories, program files, document files, data files, and hidden or system files.

Perform the following steps.

1. Ensure that the directory window displays the A:*.* file specification.

2. To limit the directory contents pane to displaying XLS files only:
    CHOOSE: View, By File Type

3. Enter the XLS file specification:
    TYPE: *.xls
    PRESS: (Enter)
    The directory contents pane now contains only XLS files, and the directory window Title bar now reads A:*.XLS.

4. To display the program files only:
    CHOOSE: View, By File Type

5. Enter the file specification to match all files:
    TYPE: *.*

6. Remove the X from all check boxes other than Programs.
    Your screen should appear similar to Figure 3.5.

Figure 3.5

The By File Type
dialog box

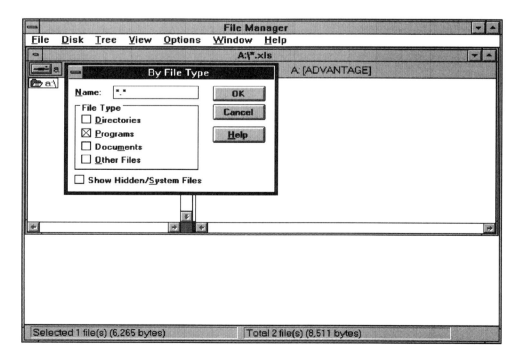

7. PRESS: [Enter] or CLICK: OK
   One file appears in the directory contents pane (PHONES.EXE).

8. To display all the files in drive A:, do the following:
   CHOOSE: View, By File Type

9. SELECT: *all check boxes except for Show Hidden/System Files*

10. PRESS: [Enter] or CLICK: OK

WORKING WITH MULTIPLE DIRECTORY WINDOWS

To facilitate copying and moving files among disk drives and directories, File Manager allows you to open multiple directory windows simultaneously. This feature enables you to see both source and target drives or directories during copy and move procedures. Multiple windows also make it easier to perform drag and drop file management.

To open a new directory window, you double-click the mouse pointer on a drive icon or choose the Window, New Window command. You can also display a new window for a specific directory by holding down the [Shift] key as you double-click the directory's folder icon. To close, minimize, or maximize a directory window, select the appropriate command from its Control menu. You close a window by double-clicking its Control menu.

You arrange open directory windows in the File Manager application window using the Window, Cascade command ([Shift]+[F5]) or the Window, Tile command ([Shift]+[F4]). Because only one directory window can be active at a time, you must select the desired window before issuing commands from the menu. To make a window active, click on the window using a mouse or press [Ctrl]+[Tab] until the Title bar of the desired window becomes a solid or different color. If a window is hidden from view or if no mouse is available, choose the Window command and then select the appropriate window from the list on the pull-down menu.

Perform the following steps to practice working with multiple windows.

1. Ensure that the directory window displays the A:*.* file specification.

2. To open a new window:
    CHOOSE: Window, New Window
    Notice that each directory window Title bar has a number attached to
    the A:*.* file specification for identification.

3. To open a new window for drive C:, do the following:
    DOUBLE-CLICK: drive C: icon (🖴c)

    CAUTION: If you single-click the drive C: icon by mistake, the active
    window changes its display to show files and directories for drive C:.
    When you double-click the icon, a third window should appear.

4. To tile the open directory windows:
    CHOOSE: Window, Tile
    Your screen should now appear similar to Figure 3.6.

Figure 3.6

Using the
Window, Tile
command

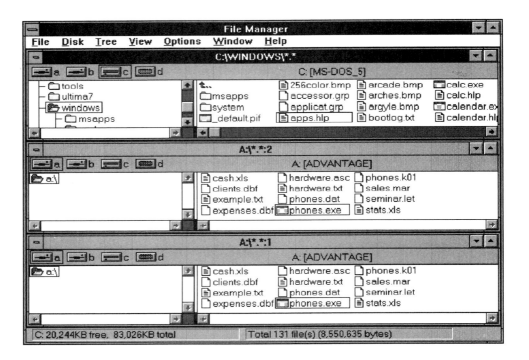

5. To cascade the windows using the keyboard:
   PRESS: [Shift]+[F5]
   The windows are layered in the application window.

6. To close the drive C: window, you first select the directory window:
   PRESS: [Ctrl]+[Tab] to cycle through the open windows
   SELECT: drive C: directory window
   (Note: You can also press [Ctrl]+[F6] to cycle through the open directory windows.)

7. PRESS: [Alt]+Hyphen
   CHOOSE: Close

8. To close the A:*.*:2 window:
   DOUBLE-CLICK: Control menu for the A:*.*:2 directory window
   Notice that the Title bar for the remaining window still reads A:*.*:1.

9. To update the information in the remaining directory window:
   CHOOSE: Window, Refresh
   The Title bar now reads A:*.* for the directory window. (Note: You can also press [F5] to refresh the screen.)

Quick Reference
Opening Multiple
Directory Windows

- To open a new window using the menu, choose the Window, New Window command.
- To open a new window for a specific disk drive, double-click the desired drive's icon.
- To open a new window for a directory, press and hold down the [Shift] key as you double-click the directory's folder icon.

Quick Reference
Arranging Multiple
Directory Windows

- To layer the open directory windows, choose Window, Cascade or press [Shift]+[F5].
- To tile the open directory windows, choose Window, Tile or press [Shift]+[F4].

COPYING AND MOVING FILES

To copy files using File Manager, you first select the desired files from the directory contents pane and then issue the File, Copy command. When prompted by the dialog box, enter the target or destination for the selected files. To move files from one location to another, you choose the File, Move command from the Menu bar. The only difference between Copy and Move is that with Move the original files are deleted.

File Manager offers a shortcut method for copying and moving files called drag and drop. After selecting files from the directory contents pane, you drag the highlighted files to their new location (for example, a folder in the directory tree pane or an icon in the drive icons area). If you drag the files to a different directory on the same drive, Windows views the mouse action as a Move command. If you drag the files to a different drive, Windows views the mouse action as a Copy command.

Perform the following steps to practice copying and moving files using the menu commands and the drag and drop feature.

1. To display two directory windows:
    CHOOSE: Window, New Window
    CHOOSE: Window, Tile

2. To display the files for drive A: in the top window and the files for drive C: in the bottom window, do the following:
    PRESS: Ctrl +a
    PRESS: Ctrl + Tab
    PRESS: Ctrl +c
    CLICK: top folder icon in the drive C: directory tree pane
    Your screen should appear similar to Figure 3.7 before continuing. (Note: Your screen display will show different filenames for drive C: than the screen graphic in Figure 3.7.)

Figure 3.7

Viewing files from
drive A: and
drive C: at the
same time

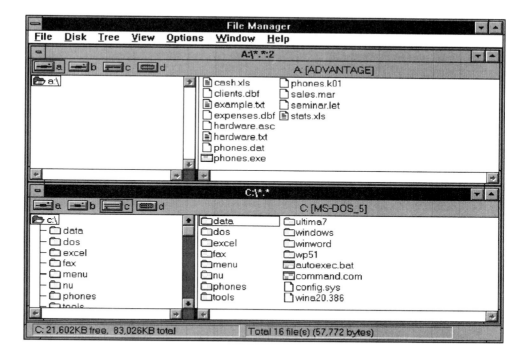

3. To select the directory contents pane for drive A:, do the following:
   PRESS: [Ctrl]+[Tab]
   PRESS: [Tab] until the Selection cursor appears in the directory contents pane for drive A:

4. SELECT: STATS.XLS file
   Ensure that the file is highlighted in reverse video before proceeding.

   CAUTION: Sometimes the Selection cursor appears as a frame around a file or directory folder without actually selecting the file or directory. When selecting files, ensure that the file is highlighted in reverse video.

5. To copy the STATS.XLS file to the root directory of drive C:, first issue the COPY command:
   CHOOSE: File, Copy
   (Note: You can also press [F8] to execute the File, Copy command.)

6. Enter the destination for the file in the dialog box:
   TYPE: c:
   PRESS: [Enter] or CLICK: OK
   The STATS.XLS file immediately appears in the directory contents pane for drive C:.

7. To move the CLIENTS.DBF file to drive C:, do the following:
    SELECT: CLIENTS.DBF file from drive A:
    CHOOSE: File, Move
    (Note: You can also press F7 to execute the File, Move command.)

8. Enter the destination for the file in the dialog box:
    TYPE: c:
    PRESS: Enter or CLICK: OK
    The CLIENTS.DBF file appears in the directory contents pane for drive C: and is removed from the directory contents pane for drive A:.

9. To copy multiple files using the drag and drop method, first select the files using the mouse:
    CLICK: HARDWARE.TXT
    PRESS: Ctrl and hold it down
    CLICK: PHONES.DAT
    CLICK: SALES.MAR

10. Release the Ctrl key. The files remain highlighted in reverse video.

11. Position the mouse pointer over one of the highlighted files.

12. CLICK: left mouse button and hold it down

13. DRAG: mouse pointer to the root directory folder in drive C:
    Position the mouse pointer directly over the top folder appearing in the directory tree pane for drive C:. (Note: You can also drop the files on the drive C: icon in the drive icons area. However, the files are copied or moved to the default directory on the drive, which may not be the desired directory. Therefore, you should drop files on the target directory folder in the directory tree pane, rather than on a drive icon.)

14. Release the mouse button.

15. If the mouse pointer was positioned correctly, a dialog box appears asking you for confirmation to copy the files to drive C:. Answer yes:
    PRESS: Enter or CLICK: Yes

    CAUTION: Ensure that the wording in the dialog box is correct before responding to the prompt. Check that the dialog box confirms the Copy or Move command and that the target location is accurate. There is not an Undo command available in the File Manager.

1. Select the files to copy or move.
2. CHOOSE: File, Copy ([F8]) or File, Move ([F7])
3. Enter the destination into the dialog box.
4. Press [Enter] or click on OK.

RENAMING FILES

To rename files using File Manager, you first select the file from the directory contents pane and then issue the File, Rename command. When prompted by the dialog box, you enter the new name for the selected file.

Perform the following steps.

1. SELECT: the directory contents pane for drive C:

2. SELECT: STATS.XLS file
   Make certain that you are selecting the file from the directory contents pane for drive C:, and not drive A:.

3. To rename the file to STATS.OLD:
   CHOOSE: File, Rename

4. Enter the new name in the dialog box:
   TYPE: stats.old
   PRESS: [Enter] or CLICK: OK
   The new filename appears in the directory contents pane.

1. Select the file or files to rename.
2. CHOOSE: File, Rename
3. Enter the new name into the dialog box.
4. Press [Enter] or click on OK.

DELETING FILES

To delete files using File Manager, you first select the files from the directory contents pane and then issue the File, Delete command or press [Delete]. When prompted by the dialog box, you confirm each deletion by pressing [Enter] or clicking the Yes command button. If you need to delete several files, the confirmation of each file can become quite tedious. Fortunately, File Manager allows you to turn off this confirmation feature.

You modify the confirmation setting using the Options, Confirmation command from the Menu bar. When the command is executed, a dialog box appears as shown in Figure 3.8. To turn off the Confirm on File Delete option, you remove the X mark from this check box. For this section, leave the Confirm on File Delete check box selected.

Figure 3.8

The Options, Confirmation dialog box

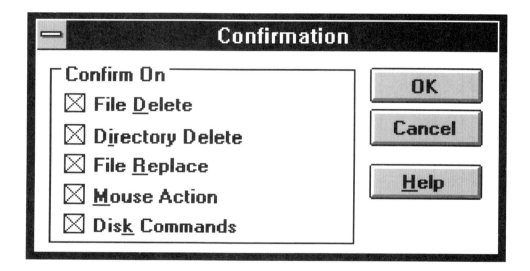

Perform the following steps.

1. SELECT: the directory contents pane for drive C:

2. SELECT: HARDWARE.TXT file in drive C:

3. To delete the file:
   CHOOSE: File, Delete
   PRESS: (Enter) or CLICK: OK to proceed with the deletion
   PRESS: (Enter) or CLICK: Yes to confirm the deletion

4. To delete several files at once, you first select all the files:
   CLICK: PHONES.DAT
   PRESS: (Ctrl) and hold it down
   CLICK: CLIENTS.DBF
   CLICK: SALES.MAR
   CLICK: STATS.OLD

5. Release the [Ctrl] key.

6. To delete the selected files:
   PRESS: [Delete]
   The filenames of the selected files appear in the dialog box.

7. When prompted, proceed with the deletion:
   PRESS: [Enter] or CLICK: OK
   CLICK: Yes to All
   The Yes to All command confirms the deletion of all selected files.

8. To close the directory window, do the following:
   DOUBLE-CLICK: the Control menu for the drive C: directory window

....

Quick Reference   1. Select the file or files to delete.
Deleting Files   2. CHOOSE: File, Delete or PRESS: [Delete]
                      3. Press [Enter] or click on OK.
                      4. When the Confirm on File Delete option is selected, you must press
                         [Enter] a second time or click on Yes to confirm the deletion.

....

MANAGING DISKS AND DIRECTORIES

A directory structure provides the foundation for hard disk management. Program and data files are organized into separate subdirectories on a hard disk to facilitate storage, retrieval, and overall file management tasks. Although software programs often create subdirectories for their program files, the creation of subdirectories for data is typically your responsibility.

File Manager eases the task of directory management. The directory tree pane displays the directory structure for the current disk drive, with the folder icons representing the individual subdirectories. To change the current directory, you select the desired folder icon in the directory tree pane. To create, rename, and remove subdirectories, you select the directory tree pane and appropriate folder icons before issuing commands from the menu.

CREATING A DIRECTORY

You create a directory using the File, Create Directory command from the menu. Before you issue the command, you must select the **parent directory** in the directory tree pane. On a blank disk, the parent directory is always the root directory or top folder icon in the tree structure.

Let's practice creating subdirectories on the Advantage Diskette.

1. Ensure that the directory window displays the A:*.* file specification with both panes visible.

2. CHOOSE: Window, Tile

3. To select the root directory of drive A:, do the following:
    CLICK: 🖿 a:\ directory folder icon in the directory tree pane

4. To create a new subdirectory under the root called WORDDATA:
    CHOOSE: File, Create Directory
    A dialog box appears for you to type the name of the new directory.

5. To create the WORDDATA directory on drive A:, do the following:
    TYPE: worddata
    PRESS: (Enter)
    Notice that a new **branch** is created in the directory tree pane.

6. To create a new directory under the root called XLDATA:
    CHOOSE: File, Create Directory
    TYPE: xldata
    PRESS: (Enter)

7. You can also create directories within directories. To demonstrate, first select the WORDDATA directory:
    CLICK: WORDDATA directory folder icon
    No files or subdirectories appear in the directory contents pane.

8. To create a subdirectory called LETTERS that branches out from the WORDDATA directory:
    CHOOSE: File, Create Directory
    TYPE: letters
    PRESS: (Enter)
    Because LETTERS is a subdirectory of WORDDATA, it is attached to the WORDDATA folder icon in the directory tree pane. The root

directory (📁a:\) is the parent directory of WORDDATA, and WORDDATA is the parent directory of LETTERS.

9. To create another subdirectory under the WORDDATA directory:
   CHOOSE: File, Create Directory
   TYPE: memos
   PRESS: (Enter)
   Notice that there are now two directory folder icons in the directory contents pane—one for LETTERS and one for MEMOS.

10. SELECT: 📁a:\ root directory folder icon
    Your screen should now appear similar to Figure 3.9.

Figure 3.9

The directory tree pane after creating directories

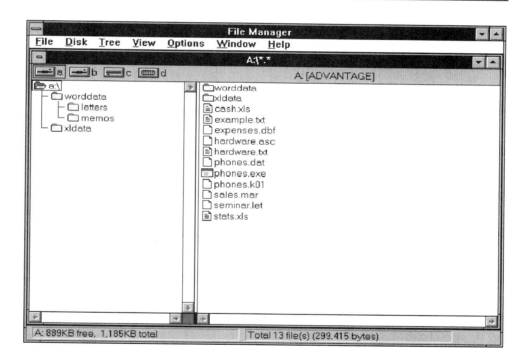

Quick Reference
Creating a New Subdirectory

1. Select the parent directory in the directory tree pane.
2. CHOOSE: File, Create Directory from the menu
3. Type the name of the new subdirectory.
4. Press (Enter) or click on OK.

SELECTING A DIRECTORY

To move to a different directory in the directory tree pane, you use the cursor-movement keys or the mouse to select the desired subdirectory folder. When you select a folder, the files within the directory are displayed in the directory contents pane. However, not all subdirectories are always displayed in the directory tree pane.

The directory tree pane is similar to an outline, where you expand or collapse topics to view more or less detail. If a directory contains subdirectories that are not currently displayed in the tree diagram, a plus sign (+) appears in the parent directory folder. A minus sign (–) in a parent directory folder tells you that all subdirectories are displayed. To display the plus and minus signs in the folder icons, you must choose the Tree, Indicate Expandable Branches command from the menu.

You expand and collapse branches in the directory tree using the keyboard, mouse, or Tree option in the Menu bar. The Tree option contains four commands for manipulating the tree diagram, as described in Table 3.4 with menu and shortcut key methods.

Table 3.4	Command	Keyboard Shortcut	Description
Tree commands			
	Expand One Level	+	Displays one additional level in the directory tree for the highlighted branch
	Expand Branch	*	Displays all subdirectory levels under the currently selected branch
	Expand All	Ctrl+*	Displays all subdirectory levels on the currently selected drive
	Collapse Branch	–	Collapses all subdirectory levels under the currently selected branch

To practice expanding and collapsing the directory tree diagram, perform the following steps.

1. Ensure that a check mark appears next to the Indicate Expandable Branches command in the Tree pull-down menu:
   CHOOSE: Tree, Indicate Expandable Branches

2. SELECT: 📁 a:\ folder in the directory tree pane
   Notice that the folder has a minus sign (–).

3. To collapse the branch using the keyboard, press the minus sign:
   PRESS: –
   Notice that the 📁 a:\ folder now has a plus sign (+), indicating that it contains subdirectories that are not currently displayed.

4. To expand the branch using the keyboard, press the plus sign:
   PRESS: +

5. To expand the WORDDATA branch using the mouse:
   DOUBLE-CLICK: + sign on the WORDDATA directory folder icon

6. To collapse the WORDDATA branch using the mouse:
   DOUBLE-CLICK: – sign on the WORDDATA directory folder icon

7. To collapse the entire directory diagram using the Tree menu option:
   SELECT: 📁 a:\ root directory folder icon
   CHOOSE: Tree, Collapse Branch

8. To expand the entire directory tree diagram using the Tree option:
   CHOOSE: Tree, Expand All

Quick Reference
Expanding and Collapsing the Directory Tree Area

CHOOSE: Tree, *command* from the Menu bar, where *command* is one of the following commands:
1. Expand One Level — Display one additional subdirectory level
2. Expand Branch — Display all subdirectory levels for a branch
3. Expand All — Display all subdirectory levels on a drive
4. Collapse Branch — Collapse subdirectory levels for a branch

Copying and Moving Files to Subdirectories

Copying and moving files among subdirectories is identical to copying and moving files between drives. You select the files that you want to copy or move and then you issue the appropriate command. As demonstrated in the following example, moving files into different directories on the same drive is easy using the drag and drop method.

To practice moving a file to a new directory, perform the following steps.

1. To move files from one directory into another, you must first select the source folder in the directory tree pane:
    SELECT: 🗁 a:\
    The files in the root directory appear in the directory contents pane.

2. To move a file from the root directory to the LETTERS subdirectory:
    SELECT: HARDWARE.ASC file in the directory contents pane

3. Position the mouse pointer over the selected file.

4. CLICK: left mouse button and hold down
    DRAG: mouse pointer over the LETTERS directory folder icon in the directory tree pane

5. When the mouse pointer is positioned directly on top of the LETTERS folder, the Selection cursor outlines the directory folder. Release the left mouse button.

6. To complete the move operation, respond affirmatively to the confirmation dialog box:
    PRESS: ⌑Enter⌑ or CLICK: Yes

Removing a Directory

You remove a subdirectory using the File, Delete command from the Menu bar or the ⌑Delete⌑ key. Make sure that you position the Selection cursor on the subdirectory folder before issuing the Delete command. Unlike using DOS to remove a directory, using File Manager provides the automatic deletion of files and subdirectories in the directory to be removed.

Perform the following steps.

1. To remove the XLDATA directory:
   SELECT: XLDATA folder icon in the directory tree pane

2. CHOOSE: File, Delete
   PRESS: [Enter] or CLICK: OK

3. As with deleting files, you can have File Manager confirm your
   intentions for deleting directories using the Options, Confirmation
   command. To confirm the directory deletion:
   PRESS: [Enter] or CLICK: Yes

4. To remove the MEMOS directory:
   SELECT: MEMOS folder in the directory tree pane
   PRESS: [Delete]
   PRESS: [Enter] or CLICK: OK to proceed with the deletion
   PRESS: [Enter] or CLICK: Yes to confirm the deletion

5. To remove the LETTERS directory:
   SELECT: LETTERS folder
   PRESS: [Delete]
   PRESS: [Enter] or CLICK: OK to proceed with the deletion
   PRESS: [Enter] or CLICK: Yes to confirm the directory deletion
   PRESS: [Enter] or CLICK: Yes to confirm the file deletion

....

Quick Reference   1. Select the subdirectory to remove in the directory tree pane.
Removing a   2. CHOOSE: File, Delete or PRESS: [Delete]
Subdirectory   3. Press [Enter] or click OK.
                        4. If the confirmation option is selected, you must press [Enter] or click
                           Yes to remove the directory.

....

RENAMING A DIRECTORY

The File, Rename command allows you to rename both files and
directories. Like most commands in File Manager, you must first select the
directory that you want renamed before issuing the command.

Perform the following steps.

1. SELECT: WORDDATA folder

2. To rename the WORDDATA directory to WPDATA:
   CHOOSE: File, Rename
   A dialog box appears for you to enter the new directory name.

3. TYPE: wpdata
   PRESS: (Enter)
   Notice that the tree diagram immediately changes to reflect the new directory name.

Quick Reference
Renaming a
Subdirectory

1. Select the subdirectory to rename in the directory tree pane.
2. CHOOSE: File, Rename
3. Type in the new name for the directory folder.
4. Press (Enter) or click OK.

PREPARING NEW DISKS

The Disk, Format Disk command formats a floppy diskette in preparation for storing data. Formatting a diskette creates the root directory and deletes any existing information on the disk. Once the Format Disk command is issued, make sure that you select the diskette drive and capacity from the dialog box, among other options shown in Figure 3.10. To proceed with formatting the diskette, press (Enter) or click on OK.

Figure 3.10

The Disk, Format
Disk dialog box

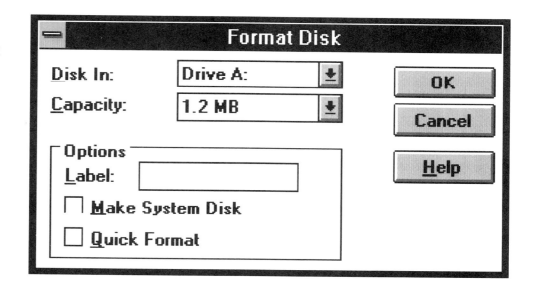

Quick Reference
Formatting a
Diskette

1. CHOOSE: Disk, Format Disk
2. Select the desired drive from the Disk In drop-down list box.
3. Select the diskette's capacity from the Capacity drop-down list box.
4. Press (Enter) or click OK.

NAMING A DISK

You can attach a name or volume label to a disk that identifies its contents, similar to an external diskette label. The Disk, Label Disk command creates, modifies, and deletes a volume label for a disk.

Perform the following steps to name the Advantage Diskette.

1. CHOOSE: Disk, Label Disk

2. TYPE: workdisk
   PRESS: (Enter) or CLICK: OK
   Notice that the volume label, located above the directory contents pane, displays the name "workdisk."

3. To change the name of the volume label to ADVANTAGE:
   CHOOSE: Disk, Label Disk

4. TYPE: `advantage`
    PRESS: (Enter) or CLICK: OK

....
Quick Reference   1. CHOOSE: Disk, Label Disk
Naming a Disk   2. Type the desired name for the disk.
                          3. Press (Enter) or click OK.
....

SUMMARY

This session introduced you to File Manager, the Windows file and directory management program. After a brief explanation of file and disk management basics, the session provided a guided tour of the primary components in the File Manager application window. The most important component is the directory window, which provides a graphical depiction of the directory tree and its contents.

The file management tasks performed in the session include customizing the display of the directory window, sorting files in the directory contents pane, and copying, moving, renaming, and deleting files. Although most commands were issued from the Menu bar, the session also introduced the drag and drop techniques for managing files. In the later part of the session, you created a directory structure, moved through the directory tree, copied files from one directory to another, removed subdirectories, and renamed a subdirectory.

Many of the commands and procedures introduced in this session appear in the Command Summary (Table 3.5).

Table 3.5	*Command*	*Description*
Command Summary	<u>V</u>iew, T<u>r</u>ee and Directory	Displays the directory tree pane and directory contents pane in the directory window
	<u>V</u>iew, Tr<u>e</u>e Only	Displays the directory tree pane only in the directory window
	<u>V</u>iew, Directory <u>O</u>nly	Displays the directory contents pane only in the directory window
	<u>V</u>iew, Sp<u>l</u>it	Adjusts the area occupied by the directory tree and directory contents panes when both are displayed
	<u>D</u>isk, <u>S</u>elect Drive	Provides a dialog box of the available drives to select and display in the directory window
	<u>V</u>iew, <u>N</u>ame	Displays the file name and extension for each file in the directory contents pane
	<u>V</u>iew, <u>A</u>ll File Details	Displays the file name, extension, size, last modification date and time, and attributes for each file in the directory contents pane
	<u>V</u>iew, <u>P</u>artial Details	Displays a dialog box from which you specify the file details to display in the directory contents pane
	<u>V</u>iew, <u>S</u>ort by Name	Sorts files in the directory contents pane by name
	<u>V</u>iew, Sort <u>b</u>y Type	Sorts files in the directory contents pane by the filename extension
	<u>V</u>iew, Sort by Si<u>z</u>e	Sorts files in the directory contents pane by size
	<u>V</u>iew, Sort by <u>D</u>ate	Sorts files in the directory contents pane by last modification date
	<u>V</u>iew, By File <u>T</u>ype	Allows you to enter a file specification and limit the display of files in the directory contents pane
	<u>W</u>indow, <u>N</u>ew Window	Opens a new window that is identical to the active directory window
	<u>W</u>indow, <u>C</u>ascade	Layers the open directory windows so that each Title bar is easily viewed and selected

	Command	Description
Table 3.5 *Continued*	Window, Tile	Tiles the open directory windows to maximize the use of the File Manager application window
	File, Copy (F8)	Copies selected files from one location to another
	File, Move (F7)	Moves selected files from one location to another
	File, Rename	Renames selected files or a directory
	File, Delete (Delete)	Deletes selected files or a directory
	File, Create Directory	Creates a new directory
	Tree, *command*	Expands and collapses the directory tree
	Tree, Indicate Expandable Branches	Displays plus and minus signs in the folder icons to represent whether subdirectories are visible
	Disk, Format Disk	Prepares or initializes a new diskette for storage
	Disk, Label Disk	Creates, changes, and deletes a drive's volume label

KEY TERMS

branch In a directory structure, a branch refers to a level in the directory tree; subdirectories branch out from the root directory.

data files Disk files that contain work created or entered using an application software program; data files are not specifically associated with an application software program in File Manager.

directory structure See *directory tree.*

directory tree The organization of subdirectories on a hard disk or floppy diskette. The root directory appears at the top of the directory tree and subdirectories branch out from the root directory.

directory window A window in the File Manager application window that contains a graphical depiction of the directory tree and its contents.

document files Disk files that contain work created or entered using an application software program recognized by Windows; document files are associated with application programs in File Manager.

drag and drop A feature of File Manager, Microsoft Windows, OS/2, and Macintosh; enables you to copy, move, print, and execute files by dragging a file's icon to a specific location using a mouse.

extension One to three characters added to a file name to aid in file identification. The file name and extension are separated by a period.

file association The process of associating a file type (extension) with an application software program. You can start an application and load a document by double-clicking an associated document file.

file specification Method of referring to a file or group of files. A file specification consists of the drive letter, directory name, file name, and extension. Wildcard characters (* and ?) are used in a file specification to refer to a general group of files.

parent directory In a directory structure, the parent directory refers to the directory in the immediately preceding level of the directory tree.

program files Disk files that contain instructions for the CPU to perform specific tasks or operations.

root directory In the hierarchy of the directory structure, the first or topmost directory is the root directory; identified by a backslash (\).

Selection cursor The highlighted bar or frame that is used to select a directory, choose files, and execute commands or programs.

Split bar The vertical line that separates the directory tree pane from the directory contents pane in the directory window. You can adjust the size of either pane by moving the Split bar.

subdirectories In the hierarchy of the directory structure, subdirectories appear beneath the root directory. Subdirectories store related program, document, and data files.

wildcard character The asterisk (*) and question mark (?) are wildcard characters. The asterisk represents a single character, a group of characters, a file name, or an extension in a file specification. The question mark represents a single character in a file specification.

EXERCISES

SHORT ANSWER

1. What are three categories of files that appear on hard disks and floppy diskettes? Define each category.
2. Name the directory where files are stored on a new disk.
3. Explain why subdirectories are important to disk management.
4. Summarize the rules for naming files.
5. Name three methods for selecting a disk drive to display in the directory window.
6. What information is displayed in the directory contents pane when you choose the View, All File Details command?
7. How do you move among multiple open windows in the File Manager application window?
8. What are two commands for arranging multiple open windows in the File Manager application window? Name their keyboard shortcuts.
9. Explain the drag and drop process for copying a file between drives.
10. What does a + (plus sign) refer to when it appears in a directory folder?

HANDS-ON

(Note: In the following exercises, you perform File Manager commands using files located on the Advantage Diskette.)

1. This exercise practices some of the file management commands that were executed in File Manager this session.
    a. Ensure that the Advantage Diskette is placed into drive A:.
    b. Open the Main group window and load File Manager.
    c. Display the files from drive A: in the directory window:
        PRESS: Ctrl +a
    d. Customize the directory window to display only the files.
    e. Sort the files in the directory window by their extensions.
    f. Display the file details for all files in the directory window.
    g. Sort the files in the directory window by size.
    h. Display the filename, date, and time—not the size or file attributes—for all files in the directory window.
    i. Sort the files by their last modification date.
        Your directory window should now appear similar to Figure 3.11.

Figure 3.11

Sorting files by last modification date

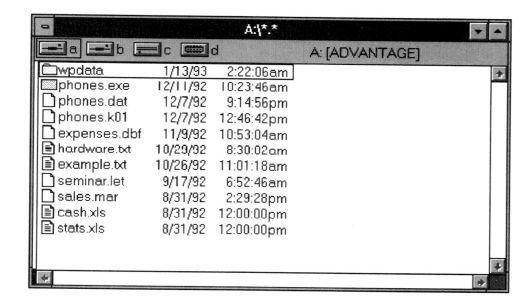

j. Limit the display of files in the directory window to files with the extension TXT. (Hint: The file specification is *.TXT).

k. Change the directory window back to the default view with the directory tree pane and the directory contents pane.

l. Change the directory contents pane back to displaying all files (*.*), sorted by name.

m. Display the file name (including extension) only in the directory contents pane.

2. This exercise practices copying, deleting, and renaming files on the Advantage Diskette.

a. With File Manager loaded, ensure that the files on the Advantage Diskette appear in the directory window.

b. Select the EXPENSES.DBF file in the directory contents pane.

c. Using the Copy command, make a backup of the EXPENSES.DBF file to a file called EXPENSES.BAK.
CHOOSE: File, Copy
TYPE: expenses.bak
CLICK: OK
The EXPENSES.BAK file appears in the directory contents pane.

d. Select the SALES.MAR file.

e. Using the keyboard shortcut method, make a backup of the SALES.MAR file to a file called SALES.BAK.
PRESS: F8
TYPE: sales.bak
PRESS: Enter
The SALES.BAK file appears in the directory contents pane.
f. Select the STATS.XLS file and the CASH.XLS file.
g. Copy these files to STATS.BAK and CASH.BAK:
PRESS: F8
TYPE: *.bak
PRESS: Enter
The asterisk is used to keep the original file names, since only the extension changes in this copy procedure.
h. Select the EXPENSES.BAK file.
i. Rename EXPENSES.BAK to EXPENSES.OLD.
CHOOSE: File, Rename
TYPE: expenses.old
CLICK: OK
j. Limit the display of files in the directory contents pane to those files with the extension BAK.
CHOOSE: View, By File Type
TYPE: *.bak
PRESS: Enter
Only the files with the extension BAK appear in the window.
k. Select all the files appearing in the directory contents pane using the keyboard shortcut:
PRESS: Ctrl +/
l. Rename all the BAK files to have the extension OLD.
CHOOSE: File, Rename
TYPE: *.old
CLICK: OK
m. Return the view to display all files on the Advantage Diskette.
CHOOSE: View, By File Type
TYPE: *.*
PRESS: Enter
n. Using a mouse, select all the files with the extension OLD.
o. Delete all the selected files.

3. This exercise practices creating a directory structure, copying files among the subdirectories, deleting files, and removing branches from the directory tree.
a. With File Manager loaded, ensure that the files on the Advantage Diskette appear in the directory window.
b. Select the root directory folder in the directory tree pane.

c. Create the directory tree appearing in Figure 3.12.

Figure 3.12

An example
directory tree

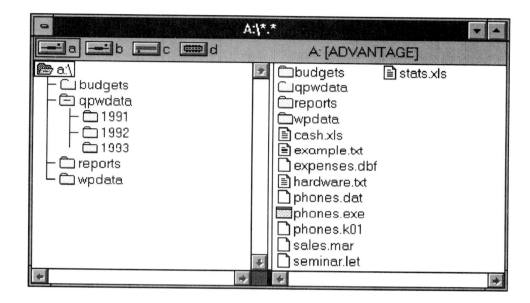

d. Select the root directory folder.
e. Collapse the branch using the keyboard.
f. Expand the branch using the mouse.
g. Collapse the QPWDATA directory using the menu.
h. Select the root directory folder.
i. Select files with the extension XLS in the directory contents pane.
j. Copy these files to the BUDGETS subdirectory:
   CHOOSE: File, Copy
   TYPE: \budgets
   PRESS: (Enter)
   Notice that the backslash refers to the root directory and the subdirectory name follows the root symbol.
k. Expand the QPWDATA directory in the directory tree pane using the mouse.
l. Select the BUDGETS directory.
m. To move the XLS files from the BUDGETS directory to the 1993 subdirectory using drag and drop, first select the two XLS files in the directory contents pane.
n. Position the mouse pointer over one of the highlighted XLS files.
o. CLICK: left mouse button and hold it down
p. DRAG: mouse pointer over top of the 1993 directory folder icon in the directory tree pane

q. Release the mouse button and confirm the move operation.
r. Remove the BUDGETS directory.
s. Remove the QPWDATA directory and all subdirectories.
t. Remove the REPORTS directory.
u. Exit File Manager.

WINDOWS 3.1: USING WRITE AND OTHER ACCESSORY PROGRAMS

You use many tools to accomplish work-related tasks. A landscaper uses a pick, shovel, and hoe to complete a garden, while an accountant uses a columnar pad, pencil, and calculator to analyze a budget. The tools that you have available often determine your productivity in a job. How productive would the landscaper or accountant be without their shovel or calculator? Microsoft understands this correlation between tools and productivity. This session introduces the accessory programs that are included with Microsoft Windows 3.1.

PREVIEW

When you have completed this session, you will be able to:

Use the Write word processing program to create, edit, format, print, and save documents.

•

Use Paintbrush to draw and manipulate graphic images.

•

Explain how to transfer data between computers.

•

Use the Clock, Calculator, Cardfile, and Calendar programs.

•

Practice mouse skills and have fun playing Solitaire.

Why Is This Session Important?
Using Write
       Creating a Document
       Saving a Document
       Opening an Existing Document
       Selecting Text in a Document
       Deleting Text
       Formatting Text
       Printing a Document
       Leaving Write
Using Paintbrush
Using Terminal
Using Clock
Using Calculator
Using Cardfile
Using Calendar
Using Character Map
Using Notepad
Playing Games
       Solitaire
       Minesweeper
Summary
       Command Summary
Key Terms
Exercises
       Short Answer
       Hands-On

WHY IS THIS SESSION IMPORTANT?

Microsoft Windows provides the working environment for application programs such as Microsoft Excel, Microsoft Word, and Aldus PageMaker. Although this graphical environment is often the principal reason for using Windows, Microsoft has included several accessory programs to make working with Windows more efficient and enjoyable. In today's world of bigger is better and more is marvelous, we commonly mistake a software program's features for a true measure of its usefulness. Why use a full-featured word processing program when the only documents that you create are one-page memos? The Windows accessories provide great utility to users who are more concerned with getting work done than comparing program features.

The Windows accessories can be divided into a few general groups: full applications, personal productivity tools, system utilities, and multimedia. In the full applications category, Windows provides the Write word processing program for creating, saving, and printing letters, memos, and other documents. With Paintbrush, you manipulate and print graphic pictures, such as maps, for inclusion in documents. Another program that is considered a full-featured application is the Terminal communications program. With Terminal, you use a modem and a regular telephone line to transfer files between computers and access on-line information systems, such as CompuServe or Prodigy.

The personal productivity tools include the Windows Clock, Calculator, Cardfile, and Calendar programs. The Windows Clock displays the current time in analog or digital format. The Calculator program provides a general or scientific calculator at your fingertips. With Cardfile, you can easily store, retrieve, and print phone and address lists. Lastly, Calendar provides an appointment book and monthly planner for organizing your time.

System utilities are programs that you use to accomplish tasks in other programs. For example, the Character Map program enables you to insert special symbols, such as a trademark or copyright symbol, into a document. With Object Packager, you create packages of objects, such as files, sounds, and graphics, for exchanging data or accessing programs from other applications. The Notepad program allows you to create, edit, save, and print ASCII text files, such as the AUTOEXEC.BAT and CONFIG.SYS system files. Lastly, the Recorder enables you to record keystrokes for later playback. With Recorder, you create macros to automate common tasks.

In the multimedia category, Windows provides Media Player and Sound Recorder. *Multimedia* is primarily used for corporate and educational presentations and is defined as the combination of different types of media, such as sound, animation, and video. With Media Player, you can play MIDI (Musical Instrument Digital Interface) sounds and control multimedia hardware devices, such as CD-ROM players. The Sound Recorder allows you to play, edit, or record sound (WAV) files. These programs require special hardware components and are not discussed in this guide.

In Sessions 4 and 5, you are introduced to several of the Windows accessories mentioned above. Although some sections provide only a brief introduction to a program, you can access their Help menu option for further on-line assistance. In this session, you perform the following tasks:

1. Insert and delete text using the Write word processing program.

2. Format, save, and print a Write document.

3. Use Paintbrush to draw a map.

4. Use Clock to display the time in analog and digital format.

5. Enter phone numbers into the Cardfile database program.

6. Make entries into the Calendar appointment book.

7. Use Notepad to compile a short reminder list.

8. Practice mouse skills by playing a game of Solitaire.

Before proceeding, make sure the following are true:

1. You have turned on your computer system and loaded Windows 3.1.
2. The Program Manager window appears on the screen.
3. Your Advantage Diskette is inserted into drive A:. You will work with files on the diskette that have been created for you. (Note: The Advantage Diskette can be duplicated by copying all of the files from your instructor's Master Advantage Diskette.)

USING WRITE

Word processing is the most commonly used application for microcomputers. Using the Windows Write word processing program, you can store, retrieve, edit, format, and print various types of documents. One significant advantage that word processing software programs have compared to typewriters is a feature called **word wrap**. Word wrap is the automatic process of moving the cursor to the next line when the end of the current line is reached. In other words, you continuously type without pressing the carriage return or (**Enter**) key to advance to the next line. In Write, the (**Enter**) key is used to end paragraphs and insert blank lines in a document.

To load Windows Write, you choose the Write program icon in the Accessories group window (discussed below). Once the program loads, you are presented with the Write window (Figure 4.1), ready for typing information or retrieving a document file.

Figure 4.1

Windows Write
word processing
program

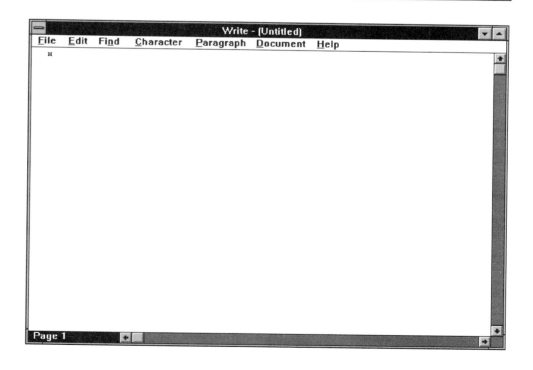

CREATING A DOCUMENT

Creating a document using Window Write is easy. You type information onto the screen, save the document to the disk, and then send it to the printer. Before entering text into the document, make sure that you have a blinking cursor (also called an **insertion point**) in the upper left-hand corner of the Write window. This marks the location where text is inserted. To the right of the cursor, you should see a small symbol called the **End mark**. Although the cursor cannot be moved below this mark, the mark automatically moves downward as you enter text.

To create a simple document, perform the following steps:

1. Open the Accessories group window and then double-click the Write program icon (✐). A blank document appears for you to begin typing.

2. TYPE: Word Processing

3. To insert a blank line between the heading and the body text:
    PRESS: ⎡Enter⎤ twice

4. TYPE: For some people the concept of writing
    using a computer is difficult to grasp. These
    people are accustomed to using the traditional
    tools for word processing -- paper and pen,
    pencil, or typewriter. It's natural to think
    that a new way of doing things is going to be
    difficult. However, once you have worked
    through this session, you'll wonder how you
    ever managed without a computer.

    (Note: If you make a mistake when you are typing the paragraph, press the ⎡BackSpace⎤ key to erase the mistake and retype the correct text. To correct previous mistakes, position the insertion point to the left of the word that you want to remove and press ⎡Delete⎤ several times until the word disappears. When you type in the new word, the existing text is pushed to the right.)

5. PRESS: ⎡Enter⎤

SAVING A DOCUMENT

When you create or edit a document, you are working in the computer's RAM (Random Access Memory). Because memory is volatile, you must save your work to a floppy diskette or hard disk for permanent storage. To save a document to a disk, select the File, Save or File, Save As command from the menu. In the resulting dialog box, type a valid file name of up to eight characters with no spaces, and then press (Enter) or click OK. Write automatically attaches an extension of WRI to the end of the file name. When the document has been saved, the name appears in the Title bar.

Perform the following steps to save the practice paragraph.

1. Ensure that the Advantage Diskette is placed into drive A:.

2. CHOOSE: File, Save As
   The File, Save and File, Save As commands are identical if the document has never been saved before. If a document has been previously saved, you use the Save command to save modifications to a document over the existing version. The Save As command is used to specify a new file name or a different disk drive for saving a file.

3. Enter the file name:
   TYPE: a:\practice
   PRESS: (Enter) or CLICK: OK
   Notice that the drive letter is placed before the file name to ensure the file is saved onto the Advantage Diskette in drive A:.

When working on an important document, you should save the document every 15 minutes to protect yourself against a surprise power outage or other catastrophe.

....

Quick Reference   1. CHOOSE: File, Save or File, Save As from the Menu bar
Saving a Document   2. If the file has never been saved before, enter a file name.
                      3. Press (Enter) or click on OK.

....

OPENING AN EXISTING DOCUMENT

To modify or print an existing document, you must first retrieve the file from storage using the File, Open command. Once the Open dialog box is displayed, type the full name of the desired document or select the document from the list box (Figure 4.2). Once the document name appears in the File Name text box, you press (Enter) or click on OK.

Figure 4.2

The File Open
dialog box

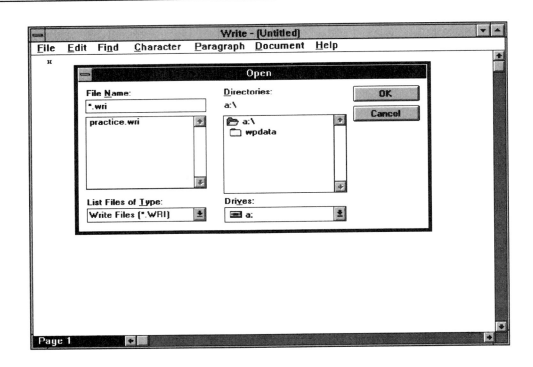

Quick Reference   1. CHOOSE: File, Open from the Menu bar
Opening an   2. Type the name of the file or select the file from the list box.
Existing Document   3. Press (Enter) or click on OK.

SELECTING TEXT IN A DOCUMENT

Once text has been typed into a document, editing and formatting changes are made by first selecting the text and then issuing the appropriate command. Selected text always appears highlighted in reverse video. In other words, selected text appears white on black if your video display is normally black on white. A selection may be comprised of letters, words, lines, paragraphs, or the entire document. When you finish formatting or editing a selection, press a cursor-movement key or click anywhere in the document to remove the highlighting from the text.

MOVING AROUND A DOCUMENT   There are better ways to move around a document than pressing the ⬆ and ⬇ cursor-movement keys. Although these keys work well in short documents, they do not provide the most efficient ways to move through long documents. Some keyboard shortcuts for moving the cursor are summarized in Table 4.1.

Table 4.1	*Keys*	*Description*
Cursor-movement commands	⬆ or ⬇	Move the cursor up or down one line
	⬅ or ➡	Move the cursor to the previous or next character
	Ctrl + ⬅	Move the cursor to the beginning of the previous word
	Ctrl + ➡	Move the cursor to the beginning of the next word
	PgUp	Move the cursor up one screen
	PgDn	Move the cursor down one screen
	Ctrl + PgUp	Move the cursor to the top of the current screen
	Ctrl + PgDn	Move the cursor to the bottom of the current screen
	Home	Move to the beginning of the current line
	End	Move to the end of the current line
	Ctrl + Home	Move to the beginning of the document
	Ctrl + End	Move to the end of the document
	F4 (GoTo)	Move to a specific page in the document

SELECTING TEXT   Write provides a column in the left margin of the document window called the **Selection area**. Although invisible, this area provides shortcuts for selecting text using the mouse. When the mouse is moved into this area, the pointer changes from an I-beam to a right-pointing diagonal arrow. Methods for selecting a word, line, paragraph, or the entire document using the mouse are summarized in Table 4.2. To extend the selection to include several words, lines, or paragraphs, make the initial selection and then hold down the left mouse button and drag the pointer over the desired text.

Table 4.2	*Select*	*Description*
Selecting text using the mouse	Single letter	Position the I-beam pointer to the left of the letter you want to select. Press down and hold the left mouse button as you drag the mouse pointer to the right.
	Single word	Position the I-beam pointer on the word and double-click the left mouse button.
	Single sentence	Hold down the Ctrl key and click once with the I-beam pointer positioned on any word in the sentence.
	Block of text	Move the cursor to the beginning of the block of text, and then position the mouse pointer I-beam at the end of the block. Hold down the Shift key and click once.
	Single line	Move the mouse pointer into the Selection area, beside the line to be selected. Wait until the pointer changes to a right-pointing diagonal arrow, and then click once.
	Single paragraph	Move the mouse pointer into the Selection area, beside the paragraph to be selected. Wait until the pointer changes to a right-pointing diagonal arrow, and then double-click.
	Entire document	Move the mouse pointer into the Selection area. Wait until the pointer changes to a right-pointing diagonal arrow, and then hold down the Ctrl key and click once.

To practice moving around a document and selecting text, perform the following steps in the PRACTICE.WRI document.

1. Move the cursor to the first line in the first paragraph.

2. To move to the end of the line:
    PRESS: [End]

3. To move to the beginning of the line:
    PRESS: [Home]

4. To select the line:
    PRESS: [Shift] and hold it down
    PRESS: [End]
    The entire line should appear highlighted.

5. Release the [Shift] key.

6. To move to the beginning of the document:
    PRESS: [Ctrl]+[Home]

7. To select the entire document:
    PRESS: [Shift] and hold it down
    PRESS: [Ctrl]+[End]

8. PRESS: [Ctrl]+[Home]

9. To select a word, position the mouse pointer over the word *concept* in the first sentence and then do the following:
    DOUBLE-CLICK: left mouse button on the word *concept*

10. To select the entire last sentence in the paragraph, position the mouse pointer over any word in the last sentence.

11. PRESS: [Ctrl] and hold it down
    CLICK: left mouse button once
    The entire sentence is selected.

12. Practice selecting text using the other methods listed in Table 4.2.

13. PRESS: [Ctrl]+[Home]

DELETING TEXT

You can delete text one character at a time using the `BackSpace` and `Delete` keys. To delete larger blocks of text, highlight the desired text and then press `Delete`. If you accidentally delete information from your document, you can easily restore it using Write's Undo feature. The Undo command allows you to reverse the last command that you performed in the document. To undo an action, select the Edit, Undo command from the menu or press `Ctrl`+z. Unfortunately, Undo only works for the last command performed, so make sure that you perform Undo immediately upon making an error.

Perform the following steps.

1. To select the first line in the practice paragraph, position the mouse pointer in the Selection area next to the first line. When the I-beam mouse pointer changes to a pointer:
   CLICK: left mouse button once

2. To delete the selected block of text:
   PRESS: `Delete`
   The highlighted block of text disappears and the remaining text flows in the paragraph to compensate for the missing line.

3. To reverse the last command:
   CHOOSE: Edit, Undo
   The text reappears in the first line.

....
Quick Reference   •   CHOOSE: Edit, Undo from the menu, or
Undo a Command   •   PRESS: `Ctrl`+z
....

FORMATTING TEXT

Formatting a document refers to applying character, paragraph, and document formatting options to text. This section describes and illustrates these three formatting options.

CHARACTER FORMATTING   Enhancing text is referred to as character formatting. Specifically, character formatting involves selecting typefaces, font sizes, and styles for text. Some of the styles available in Write include bold, italic, underline, superscript, and subscript. Write's character formatting commands are accessed through the Character menu option. When a formatting style is active, a check mark appears beside the command on the pull-down menu. Also note that some commands on the menu have keyboard shortcuts.

PARAGRAPH FORMATTING   Paragraph formatting involves changing indentation, alignment, line spacing, and tab settings for a paragraph. Paragraph and document formatting commands are accessible from the Paragraph menu option and from a special document tool called the Ruler. To display the Ruler, you choose the Document, Ruler On command from the menu. When the Ruler is displayed, the command becomes Document, Ruler Off on the pull-down menu. Using a mouse, you can easily indent paragraphs, set tab stops, and even change the margins by dragging symbols on the Ruler line. The Ruler buttons, described in Table 4.3, provide quick access to all the commands found on the Paragraph menu.

Table 4.3	*Name*	*Button*	*Description*
Ruler buttons	Left tab		Positions a left-aligned tab stop on the Ruler
	Decimal tab		Positions a decimal tab on the Ruler for aligning numbers and right aligning text
	Single space		Single-spaces the selected paragraph
	1.5-line-space		Spaces the selected paragraph by 1.5 lines
	Double space		Double-spaces the selected paragraph
	Left align		Aligns text at the left margin but provides jagged right edges as a typewriter does
	Center align		Centers the line or paragraph between the left and right margins
	Right align		Positions text flush against the right margin
	Justify		Aligns text columns at the left and right margins, similar to the paragraphs in this guide

DOCUMENT FORMATTING   Document formatting refers to the creation, insertion, and modification of headers, footers, page numbers, margins, and tab settings in a document. A document **header** and **footer** can appear at the top and bottom of each page. The header often contains the title or heading for a document while the footer shows the page numbers or copyright information. You choose the Document, Header command or the Document, Footer command to create a header or a footer for a document. The Document, Page Layout command enables you to specify the top, bottom, left, and right margins for the printed document.

Perform the following steps to practice the character, paragraph, and document formatting commands.

1. Ensure that PRACTICE.WRI appears in the Write document window.

2. To practice enhancing text, select the word "difficult" in the first sentence, and then do the following:
   CHOOSE: Character, Bold
   The selection is made bold and the text remains highlighted.

3. To italicize the same word using a keyboard shortcut:
   PRESS: ⌨Ctrl+i
   The selection is now italicized and bold.

4. To underline the term "word processing" in the second sentence, select the text and then do the following:
   CHOOSE: Character, Underline

5. To make the heading text "Word Processing" bold and underlined, select the text and then do the following:
   PRESS: ⌨Ctrl+b
   PRESS: ⌨Ctrl+u

6. To perform paragraph formatting commands, you should first display the Ruler line:
   CHOOSE: Document, Ruler On

7. To center the heading text:
   CHOOSE: Paragraph, Centered
   The heading is centered between the margins.

8. Position the cursor anywhere in the paragraph.

9. CLICK: Justify button in the Ruler

10. To modify the margin settings for the document:
    CHOOSE: Document, Page Layout

11. Set the left and right margins to 1.5 inches:
    PRESS: Tab
    TYPE: 1.5
    PRESS: Tab
    TYPE: 1.5
    PRESS: Enter or CLICK: OK
    Notice that the symbols on the Ruler line have moved to show the new margin settings.

12. Save the document and overwrite the existing version on the Advantage Diskette:
    CHOOSE: File, Save
    Your screen should now appear similar to Figure 4.3.

Figure 4.3

Formatting the PRACTICE.WRI document

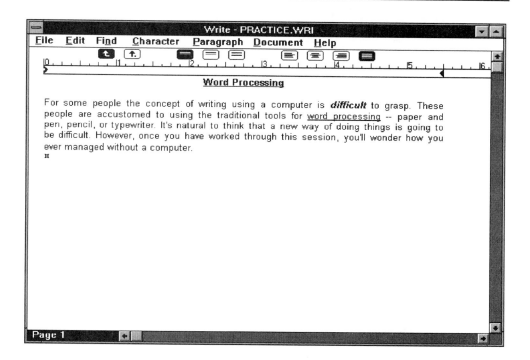

Quick Reference
Character
Formatting

1. Select the text to format.
2. CHOOSE: Character from the Menu bar
3. Select a character formatting option from the pull-down menu.

Quick Reference *Paragraph* *Formatting*	1. Position the cursor in the paragraph to be formatted, or select several paragraphs using the mouse or keyboard. 2. CHOOSE: Paragraph from the Menu bar 3. Select a paragraph formatting option from the pull-down menu, or click on the appropriate symbol in the Ruler.

Quick Reference *Document* *Formatting*	• To create a header for a document, choose Document, Header. • To create a footer for a document, choose Document, Footer. • To specify the margin settings, choose Document, Page Layout.

PRINTING A DOCUMENT

Before sending a document to the printer, you choose the File, Repaginate command to have Write renumber the pages in the document. To print the document, choose the File, Print command. With Write, you can print a selected area of text, only certain pages, or the entire document. Make a selection from the Print Range area and then press (Enter) or click on OK.

Perform the following steps.

1. To print the practice paragraph:
   CHOOSE: File, Print
   Because the document is only one paragraph in length, you do not need to repaginate the file before printing.

2. Ensure that the All option is selected in the Print Range area.

3. PRESS: (Enter) or CLICK: OK
   The document is sent to the printer.

Quick Reference *Printing a* *Document*	1. CHOOSE: File, Print from the Menu bar 2. Specify what to print in the Print Range area. 3. Press (Enter) or click on OK.

LEAVING WRITE

When you are finished using Windows Write, save your work and exit the program. If you have made modifications to a file and have not yet saved the changes, Write will ask whether the file should be saved or abandoned before exiting the program.

Perform the following steps.

1. To exit Write:
    CHOOSE: File, Exit

2. If you have made any modifications to the current document, a dialog box appears. To abort the modifications and exit:
    SELECT: No

....

Quick Reference   1. CHOOSE: File, Exit from the Menu bar
Exiting Write   2. If necessary, respond to the prompts for saving or aborting the
                             current document, or cancel the command altogether.

....

USING PAINTBRUSH

The Paintbrush accessory program enables you to create, modify, and save graphic pictures, including drawings, scanned images, and screen captures. You can print these graphics directly from Paintbrush or you can paste them into documents created using other applications, such as Microsoft Word for Windows or Aldus PageMaker. To load Paintbrush, you double-click the Paintbrush program icon in the Accessories group window. Once the program loads, you are presented with a blank canvas for creating a new picture or retrieving an existing graphic file.

The Paintbrush application window (Figure 4.4) consists of the following components: Tool Box, Line Width Area, Color Palette, and Canvas. The Tool Box is located in the two columns at the left-hand side of the window and contains icons for drawing and filling shapes, typing text, erasing elements, and moving parts of a drawing. The Line Width Area appears beneath the Tool Box and lets you change the width of all tools that produce lines. The Palette is displayed across the bottom of the screen. In a color picture, Paintbrush provides a color palette. In a monochrome picture, Paintbrush provides a pattern palette. You choose a foreground color/pattern by pointing at the desired option and clicking the left mouse button. You select a background color/pattern by pointing at the desired option and clicking the right mouse button.

Figure 4.4

The Paintbrush
application window

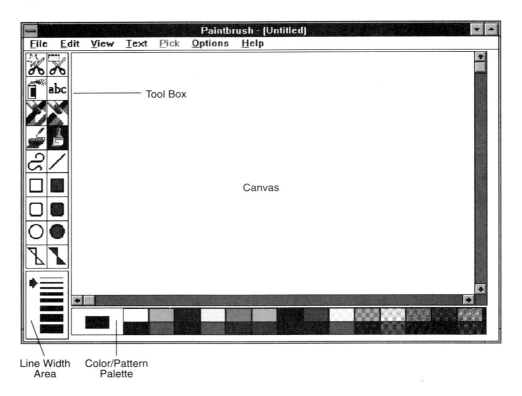

Line Width   Color/Pattern
   Area   Palette

When you first load Paintbrush, the Brush tool is chosen by default. To change the selected tool, you click on the desired icon in the Tool Box. Table 4.4 provides a description of all the tools in the Tool Box.

Table 4.4	*Name*	*Icon*	*Description*
Tool Box icons	Scissors		Cuts a portion of the drawing for moving or deletion
	Pick		Cuts a rectangular portion of the drawing for moving or deletion
	Airbrush		Spray paints the current color onto the canvas
	Text tool	abc	Enters text
	Color Eraser		Erases text or graphics that use the currently selected color
	Eraser		Erases all text or graphics regardless of color
	Paint Roller		Fills a shape with the currently selected color
	Brush		Draws with the current color
	Curve		Creates a curved line
	Line		Draws a straight line
	Box		Draws an empty box
	Filled Box		Draws a box filled with the current color
	Rounded Box		Draws an empty box with rounded edges
	Filled Rounded Box		Draws a box with rounded edges filled with the current color
	Circle/Ellipse		Draws an empty circle or ellipse

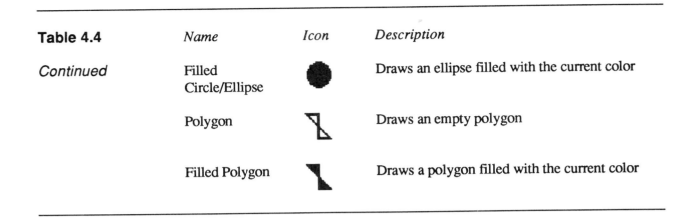

Table 4.4	*Name*	*Icon*	*Description*
Continued	Filled Circle/Ellipse		Draws an ellipse filled with the current color
	Polygon		Draws an empty polygon
	Filled Polygon		Draws a polygon filled with the current color

Perform the following steps to create the map that appears in Figure 4.5.

1. To load Paintbrush, open the Accessories group window and then double-click the Paintbrush program icon.

Figure 4.5

Drawing a map using Paintbrush

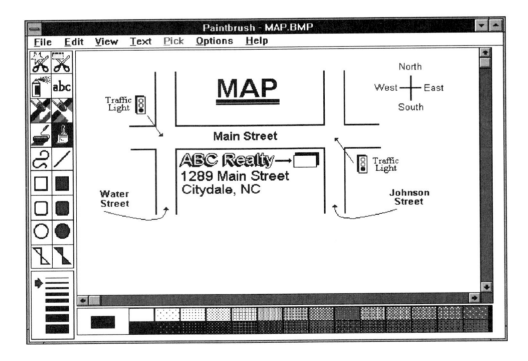

2. To draw Main Street, use the Line tool:
   CLICK: Line tool

3. Position the cross hair on the canvas at the west end of the road.

4. CLICK: left mouse button and hold it down
   DRAG: cross-hair mouse pointer to the east end of the road

5. Release the mouse button to complete the line.

6. Using the same steps that you used to create the initial line, use the Line, Box, Filled Box, Circle, Filled Circle, Text, and Eraser tools to complete the rest of the map.

7. To save the map:
   CHOOSE: File, Save As
   TYPE: map
   PRESS: Enter or CLICK: OK

Learning to create a graphic takes many hours of practice and patience. For more information on Paintbrush, choose the Help option in the Menu bar.

Using Terminal

The Terminal accessory program enables you to communicate with another computer or a communication service, such as CompuServe or Prodigy. In addition to the Terminal software, you require a **modem** to successfully communicate across telephone lines. For example, if you want to send a file to an associate, you both require modems to complete the file transfer. If your computers reside in the same office, you can connect your computers using a null modem cable instead of a modem. Regardless of the type of hardware used to make the connection, you both require a software program, such as Terminal, to complete the communication link.

To start a Terminal session, you double-click the Terminal program item in the Accessories group window. Before you can exchange information with another computer, you must ensure that the software settings, listed below, are identical for each computer.

Baud Rate	The speed of data transfer, as limited by the modem. The most common rates are 1200, 2400, and 9600. (Pronounced "Bod Rate.")
Data Bits	Data is transferred in packets across the telephone line or null modem cable. This setting specifies the number of data bits in a packet, typically 7 or 8.

Stop Bits	The timing units or spaces between transmitted characters; usually 1.
Parity	A form of error checking. If you select 8 data bits, you must select no parity.
Flow-Control	Method of telling the transmitter that the receiving buffer is full and cannot accept any more data.

In Terminal, you select the Settings, Communications command to modify these parameters in the Communications dialog box (Figure 4.6). Once they are modified, you can save the settings to a disk file by choosing File, Save As and entering a file name. To exit Terminal, choose File, Exit.

Figure 4.6

Setting the communications parameters in Terminal

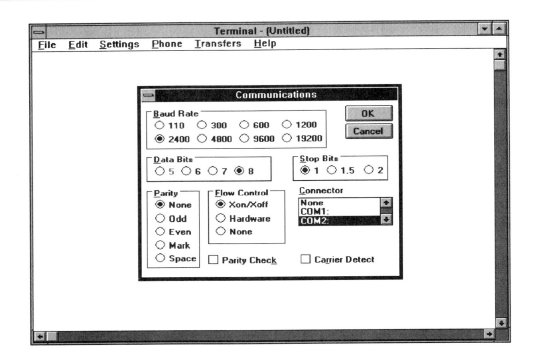

USING CLOCK

The Windows Clock program displays the date and time from your computer's internal clock. Clock has two options for displaying the time: analog and digital. When you launch the Clock program from the Accessories window, an analog clock appears on the screen. If you want to display a digital clock face, choose the Settings, Digital command. If you want the current date displayed in the window as well, choose Settings, Date. Other options in the Settings pull-down menu allow you to change the display font, hide the Title bar, or suppress the seconds from being shown. To have the Clock window float above all other open windows (even when it is not the active window), choose the Always on Top command from the Clock's Control menu.

Perform the following steps to load the Windows Clock program.

1. Open the Accessories group window and double-click the Clock program icon.

2. To specify a digital clock face:
   CHOOSE: Settings, Digital

3. To specify an analog clock face:
   CHOOSE: Settings, Analog

4. To display the date in the clock window, ensure that a check mark appears next to the Date command in the Settings pull-down menu:
   CHOOSE: Settings, Date
   Notice that the date is displayed in the Title bar.

5. CHOOSE: Settings, Digital
   Notice that the date is displayed in the clock window.

6. Maximize Clock to fill the entire screen.

7. Minimize Clock to an icon. When the clock appears as an icon on the Desktop, it continues to display the correct time.

8. Restore Clock to a window and then size the window to measure approximately 3- by 5-inches, similar to an index card.

9. To remove the Title bar and display only the clock face:
   CHOOSE: Settings, No Title

10. Move Clock around the Desktop by dragging the clock face.

11. To redisplay the Title bar:
    DOUBLE-CLICK: clock face

12. Minimize Clock to an icon.

....

Quick Reference • To display a digital clock face, choose Settings, Digital.
Customizing • To display an analog clock face, choose Settings, Analog.
Clock's Display • To display the date in the clock window, choose Settings, Date.
• To remove the display of the Title bar, choose Settings, No Title.
• To ensure that the clock always layers other windows, choose
  Always on Top from Clock's Control menu.

....

USING CALCULATOR

The Windows Calculator provides a general and scientific version of a standard desktop calculator. You use Calculator to perform quick calculations while working in other application programs. For example, you could use Calculator to multiply an invoice amount by a tax rate when creating an invoice in Write. The results of any calculation can be copied to the Windows Clipboard for pasting into other documents or applications. To load Calculator, you select the Calculator program icon in the Accessories group window.

Perform the following steps to load Calculator.

1. Open the Accessories group window and then double-click the Calculator program icon.

2. By default, Calculator first displays the general or standard version. To display the scientific version:
   CHOOSE: View, Scientific

3. To redisplay the general version:
   CHOOSE: View, Standard

4. To perform a simple calculation, use the mouse to click numbers and symbols on the standard calculator keypad:
    CLICK: 8
    CLICK: *
    CLICK: 9
    CLICK: =
    The result, 72, appears in the display area.

5. To copy this value to the Clipboard:
    CHOOSE: Edit, Copy

6. To enter a new calculation, clear the last calculation from memory:
    CLICK: C button under the display area
    (Note: You can also press (Esc) to clear the calculation.)

7. Enter a new calculation:
    TYPE: 220/13*42
    TYPE: =
    The result, 710.7692307692, is displayed.

8. To exit the Calculator program:
    DOUBLE-CLICK: Control menu

....

Quick Reference
Copying the
Results of a
Calculation to the
Clipboard

1. Open the Accessories group window and double-click the Calculator program icon.
2. Using the mouse or keyboard, enter the calculation and press the equal sign to display the result.
3. To copy the result to the Clipboard, choose the Edit, Copy command from the menu.
4. To close the Calculator, double-click its Control menu.

....

USING CARDFILE

The Cardfile program lets you automate your filing system. It enables you to store and retrieve information, such as phone numbers and recipes, using electronic 3- by 5-inch index cards. To launch Cardfile, you select the Cardfile program icon in the Accessories group window.

With Cardfile, you store related information in disk files. For example, you may have one file called PERSONAL that contains phone numbers for your personal contacts and another file called BUSINESS for your business contacts. After adding or modifying index cards in a file, you save the file to the disk using the File, Save command. To use the index cards at a later date, choose File, Open from the menu, select the desired card file, and press (Enter) or click on OK.

In the Cardfile application window, you display information using either the Card view or the List view. The Card view shows all the information for the top index card and layers the remaining cards behind. Each index card consists of an index line at the top of the card and an information area. Cardfile sorts the cards based on your entry in the index line; usually a name. The information area can contain various types of data, including text, pictures, or sound recordings. The List view displays the index line of each card in a report format—perfect for printing out a quick summary of a file. Cardfile displays the current view and number of cards on the Status line, located below the Menu bar.

Perform the following steps to create a phone book using Cardfile.

1. Open the Accessories group window and then double-click the Cardfile program icon.

2. When you first load Cardfile, a new file appears with one blank card displayed in the application window. To create a card file, you simply begin adding index cards to the file:
    CHOOSE: Edit, Index to modify the index line on the first blank card
    (Note: You can also press (F6) or double-click in the index line using the mouse to modify an index entry.)

3. TYPE: `Veiner, Sima`
    PRESS: (Enter) or CLICK: OK
    The text appears in the index line of the first card.

4. Enter some information for Sima Veiner:
    TYPE: `Chicago, IL`
    PRESS: (Enter)
    TYPE: `312-654-9871`

5. To add a new card:
    CHOOSE: Card, Add
    (Note: You can also press (F7) to quickly add a new card.)

6. TYPE: Sagi, Janos
   PRESS: [Enter] or CLICK: OK

7. Enter some information for Janos:
   TYPE: Boston, MA
   PRESS: [Enter]
   TYPE: 617-552-4224

8. PRESS: [F7] to add another card

9. TYPE: McFee, Becky
   PRESS: [Enter] or CLICK: OK
   TYPE: Toronto, ON
   PRESS: [Enter]
   TYPE: 416-559-1080
   Notice that the cards are placed in alphabetical order.

10. To scroll through the cards:
    CLICK: left and right scroll arrows in the Status line
    (Note: Using a keyboard, you can press the [PgUp] and [PgDn] keys to scroll through the cards.)

11. To display the card file using List view:
    CHOOSE: View, List

12. To save the card file to the Advantage Diskette:
    CHOOSE: File, Save As
    TYPE: a:\personal
    PRESS: [Enter] or CLICK: OK
    Windows automatically adds the extension CRD to the file name.

13. To print the cards as they are displayed in Card view:
    CHOOSE: View, Card
    CHOOSE: File, Print All
    (Note: You can print a single card by choosing File, Print.)

14. To exit Cardfile:
    CHOOSE: File, Exit

Quick Reference   •   To edit the index line, choose Edit, Index or press F6 .
Using Cardfile   •   To add a new card, choose Card, Add or press F7 .
                        •   To display the cards in List view, choose View, List.
                        •   To display the cards in Card view, choose View, Card.
                        •   To print all the cards, choose File, Print All.
                        •   To print the current card, choose File, Print.
                        •   To save the card file, choose File, Save As.
                        •   To exit Cardfile, choose File, Exit.

USING CALENDAR

Windows provides you with a Calendar program for maintaining an on-line appointment book. When you select the Calendar program icon in the Accessories group window, an empty appointment calendar appears. You can use this calendar to enter new appointments or retrieve a calendar file that you have previously saved to the disk. Like a normal appointment book, you enter information in the appropriate time slots. At the bottom of the window, Calendar provides a scratch pad that you can use to enter notes or reminders while working in the diary. To access the scratch pad, you click in the area using a mouse or press the Tab key.

In the application window, you can display either a daily appointment book (Figure 4.7) or a monthly calendar. To display a single day in the appointment book, choose the View, Day command. To view an entire calendar month, choose View, Month from the menu. Calendar displays the computer's internal date and time on the Status line, located below the Menu bar.

Figure 4.7

Calendar program:
Day view

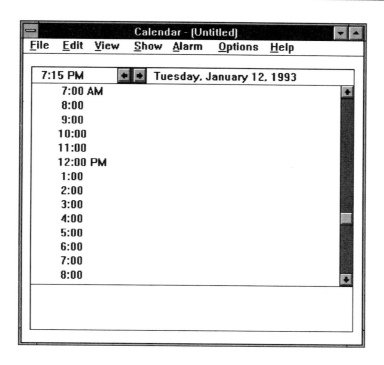

To move forward or backward one day in the appointment book, you click
the right or left scroll arrows in the Status line. Using the keyboard, you
access the Show menu and then choose Today, Previous, Next, or Date
from the pull-down menu. Calendar provides several additional features for
your appointment book, such as sounding an alarm to warn you of
upcoming appointments. You can also print your appointments using the
File, Print command. For further assistance, choose the Help option in the
Menu bar.

Perform the following steps to load Calendar.

1. Open the Accessories group window and then double-click the
   Calendar program icon. A diary page in an empty appointment book
   appears on the screen.

2. In the appointment area, place an entry at 12:00 PM (noon):
   CLICK: 12:00 PM
   Notice that a flashing insertion point appears to the right of 12:00 PM.

3. TYPE: Lunch meeting with Carlos.

4. You can have Calendar remind you of an appointment by setting an alarm:
CHOOSE: Alarm, Set
A small bell symbol appears beside the appointment. (Note: You can also press F5 to set an alarm.)

5. Because it takes 10 minutes to walk to the restaurant, you would like Calendar to prompt you at 11:50 AM for your 12:00 PM appointment:
CHOOSE: Alarm, Controls

6. To specify an early ring in minutes:
TYPE: 10
PRESS: Enter or CLICK: OK

7. To set a second appointment for 2:13 PM:
CHOOSE: Options, Special Time
TYPE: 2:13
CLICK: PM option button
PRESS: Enter or CLICK: Insert
The new time appears in the appointment book. (Note: You can also press F7 to insert a special time.)

8. TYPE: Send proposal to Bermuda using Terminal.

9. To view the next day's appointments:
CLICK: right scroll arrow in the Status line
(Note: To move to the next day, you can also press Ctrl+PgDn or choose Show, Next from the menu.)

10. To move back one day in the appointment book:
PRESS: Ctrl+PgUp
(Note: To move to the previous day, you can also click the left scroll arrow in the Status line or choose Show, Previous from the menu.)

11. To display a monthly calendar view of the appointment book:
CHOOSE: View, Month

12. To view the appointment book for any date:
DOUBLE-CLICK: *any date box*

13. To quickly switch between the views:
DOUBLE-CLICK: Date in the Status line to toggle the view
DOUBLE-CLICK: Date in the Status line to toggle the view again

14. To save the appointment book:
    CHOOSE: File, Save As
    TYPE: a:\mydiary
    PRESS: (Enter) or CLICK: OK
    Windows automatically adds the extension CAL to the file name.

15. To exit Calendar:
    CHOOSE: File, Exit

Quick Reference
Using Calendar

- To display the appointment book, choose View, Day.
- To display the monthly calendar, choose View, Month.
- To display the next appointment date, choose Show, Next.
- To display the previous appointment date, choose Show, Previous.
- To display today's appointment book, choose Show, Today.
- To specify a special time, choose Options, Special Time.
- To set an alarm, choose Set, Alarm.
- To print appointments according to date, choose File, Print.
- To save the calendar file, choose File, Save or File, Save As.
- To exit Calendar, choose File, Exit.

USING CHARACTER MAP

The Character Map program enables you to insert special characters, such as a trademark or copyright symbol, into a document. To load Character Map, you select its program icon in the Accessories group window. The dialog box appears showing the available characters for the selected font. To display other characters and symbols, select another font from the Font list box. Using the mouse or the keyboard, highlight the desired symbol from the Character Map dialog box and choose the Select command button. Once selected, you can copy the character to the Clipboard by selecting the Copy command button. From the Clipboard, you paste the character into a document, spreadsheet, or other application program.

Perform the following steps to copy a character to the Clipboard.

1. Open the Accessories group window and then double-click the Character Map program icon. The dialog box in Figure 4.8 appears for you to choose a symbol.

Figure 4.8

The Character Map
dialog box

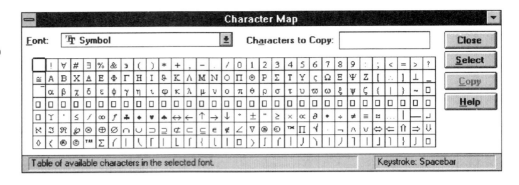

2. In the Font drop-down list box, select the Times New Roman TrueType (T$_T$) font to display the characters and symbols for that set.

3. To temporarily enlarge a symbol, position your mouse pointer over a symbol in the map area and then do the following:
   CLICK: left mouse button and hold it down

4. Select the Symbol TrueType (T$_T$) font from the Font list box to display a new set of characters and symbols.

5. CLICK: left mouse button and hold it down
   DRAG: mouse pointer over the map to enlarge the symbols

6. Select the Wingdings TrueType (T$_T$) font to display another new set of characters and symbols.

7. Select any symbol by clicking on it in the map.

8. To copy the highlighted symbol to the Clipboard for pasting into other documents:
   SELECT: Select command button
   SELECT: Copy command button
   The character symbol is placed onto the Clipboard.

9. To close the Character Map dialog box:
   SELECT: Close command button

1. Open the Accessories group window and double-click the Character
   Map program icon.
2. Select a font from the Font drop-down list box.
3. Highlight a symbol from the Character Map dialog box.
4. To copy the symbol to the Clipboard, select the Select command
   button and then the Copy command button.
5. To close the dialog box, select the Close command button.

USING NOTEPAD

As a text editor, the Windows Notepad program does not provide
sophisticated word processing capabilities like those available in Windows
Write. With Notepad, you create, save, and print batch files (BAT), system
files (SYS), and other **ASCII** text files (unformatted files containing
characters from the American Standard Code for Information Interchange).
It is designed primarily to create simple text files consisting of line item
entries. You start Notepad by selecting its program icon from the
Accessories group window.

Perform the following steps to create a text file using Notepad.

1. Open the Accessories group window and double-click the Notepad
   program icon. After Notepad loads into memory, a cursor appears in
   the top left-hand corner of the screen.

2. TYPE: list
   The cursor appears one character to the right of "list."

3. To move the cursor back to the beginning of the line:
   PRESS: (Home)

4. TYPE: to do
   PRESS: Space Bar
   As you type, the existing information is pushed to the right.

5. To move the cursor to the end of the line:
   PRESS: (End)

6. To add a couple of blank lines:
   PRESS: (Enter) twice

7. TYPE: 1. Pick up laundry
   PRESS: `Enter`

8. TYPE: 2. Go shopping
   PRESS: `Enter`

9. TYPE: 3. Finish reading book
   PRESS: `Enter`

10. To move to the top of the file:
    PRESS: `Ctrl`+`Home`

11. To save the file:
    CHOOSE: File, Save As
    TYPE: a:\todolist
    PRESS: `Enter` or CLICK: OK
    Notepad saves the file to the Advantage Diskette and automatically appends an extension of TXT to the file name. Notice that the Title bar at the top of the screen now displays the name of the file.

12. To exit Notepad:
    CHOOSE: File, Exit

Notice that Notepad uses keystrokes and commands similar to those in Windows Write. For more information on Notepad, access the Help menu option.

PLAYING GAMES

Windows provides two games, Solitaire and Minesweeper, for enjoyment and for bettering your mouse skills. To start either game, you must first open the Games group window. Once the group window is open, double-click the mouse pointer on the desired program icon or highlight the icon using the cursor-movement keys and press `Enter`.

SOLITAIRE

Solitaire is a computer version of the popular card game called Klondike. The objective of the game is to place the deck of 52 cards in four suit stacks at the top of the playing board. To do so, you first arrange the cards in descending order, using alternating colors (hearts or diamonds and spades or clubs). You build upon each of the original seven piles using cards from the other piles and the deck. To score points, you place cards in the suit stacks in ascending order, starting with an Ace. When all cards appear in their respective suit stack, you have won the game. Figure 4.9 shows the Solitaire playing board in the middle of a game.

Figure 4.9

The Solitaire
playing board

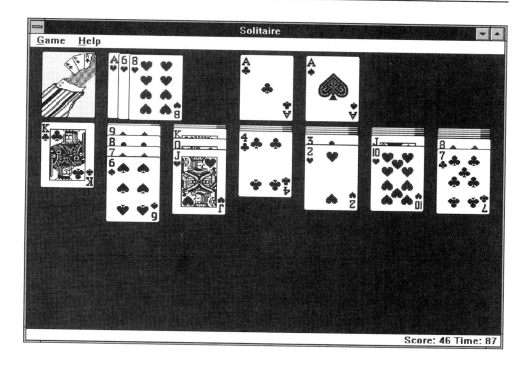

This game practices clicking, double-clicking, and dragging cards on the playing board. To load Solitaire, open the Games group window and double-click the Solitaire program icon. To flip through the deck, you click the mouse pointer on the top card in the deck. To place a card in the suit stack, you double-click the card on the playing board. To arrange cards from different piles (or from the deck) below a card pile, you drag the card or cards using the mouse. For further assistance, access the Help option in the Menu bar. To quit Solitaire, choose Game, Exit from the menu.

MINESWEEPER

Minesweeper requires strategy and luck to clear the playing board of mines. Using the mouse, you click on squares in the playing field to locate the mines. The total number of mines appears on the left side of the scoreboard and a clock appears on the right side. Through elimination, your mission is to uncover all the squares that do not contain mines.

To start Minesweeper, double-click the Minesweeper program icon in the Games group window. The board appears on the screen with all squares covered. The happy face symbol in the middle of the score board is the Restart button—you click it to restart the game. When you click a square, two events can occur: you survive or you die. If you click a square that does not contain a mine, the square will show a number that is a tally of the mines bordering that square. If you click a square that contains a mine, you lose the game. To quit Minesweeper, choose Game, Exit from the menu.

For further information about Minesweeper, access the Help menu option.

SUMMARY

This session introduced you to some of the tools that accompany the Windows graphical environment. In addition to several system utility programs, Windows provides a feature-rich word processing program called Write, a drawing package called Paintbrush, and the Terminal communications program. There are also four personal productivity programs called Clock, Calculator, Cardfile, and Calendar. In this session, you created, edited, formatted, and printed a document in Write, performed calculations using Calculator, created a personal phone book in Cardfile, and made entries into a Calendar appointment book.

Some of the commands and procedures introduced in this session appear in the Command Summary (Table 4.5).

	Command	Description
Table 4.5 Command Summary	File, New	Creates a new file to use in an application program; most applications present a new file when they are first loaded into memory
	File, Open	Retrieves a file from the disk to use in an application
	File, Save	Saves a document, drawing, card file, or calendar file
	File, Save As	Saves a document, drawing, card file, or calendar file under a new name
	File, Print	Prints a document, drawing, card file report, appointment book, or other type of document
	File, Exit	Leaves an application program
	Character, *command*	In Write, formats and enhances text using boldface, italic, underlines, and fonts
	Paragraph, *command*	In Write, formats a paragraph's alignment and line spacing
	Document, *command*	In Write, formats the document using headers and footers; defines page layout options, such as margins
	Settings, Communications	In Terminal, specifies the communications parameters, such as baud rate, data bits, stop bits, and parity
	Settings, *command*	In Clock, specifies an analog or digital clock face and the information to be displayed in the Clock window
	View, *command*	In Calculator, toggles between Standard and Scientific In Cardfile, toggles between Card and List views In Calendar, toggles between Day and Month views

KEY TERMS

ASCII   Acronym for American Standard Code for Information Interchange. An ASCII text file refers to an unformatted text file that is viewed or edited using DOS or the Notepad accessory program.

End mark   The symbol that appears at the end of a Write document. You cannot move the cursor beyond this mark.

footer   Descriptive text that appears at the bottom of each page in a document. The footer usually contains page numbers and copyright information.

header   Descriptive text that appears at the top of each page in a document. The header usually contains titles or headings.

insertion point   The vertical flashing bar in Write that indicates your current position in the document (also referred to as a cursor). The insertion point shows where the next typed characters will appear.

modem   A device for transferring information between computers using telephone lines; translates digital signals from a computer into analog signals for transmission and then back into digital signals again for processing. (A modem must be hooked up at each end of the transmission.) Modem stands for MOdulate/DEModulate.

Selection area   The leftmost column in the Write document window. The Selection area provides shortcut methods for selecting text using the mouse.

word wrap   When the cursor reaches the right-hand margin of a line, it automatically wraps to the left margin of the next line; the user does not have to press a carriage return key at the end of each line to move the cursor down.

EXERCISES

SHORT ANSWER

1. What is *multimedia*?
2. In Write, what is the Selection area?
3. What are the three levels of formatting in Write?
4. How does the Ruler assist you in formatting a document?
5. In Write, what should you do before sending a document to the printer?
6. What are the four main components of the Paintbrush screen?
7. Name two methods for connecting computers in order to transfer files.
8. How can you keep the Clock from being overlaid by other application windows on the Desktop?
9. Name three fonts that you selected in this session for displaying symbols in the Character Map dialog box.
10. How does the Notepad accessory program differ from Write?

HANDS-ON

(Note: In the following exercises, you perform Windows commands using files located on the Advantage Diskette.)

1. Using the Write word processing program, create the document appearing in Figure 4.10. Make sure to include your name in the closing of the letter. Save this document onto the Advantage Diskette as LETTER.

Figure 4.10

LETTER
document

August 28, 1993

Ms. Juanita Pallos
2910 S.W. Marine Drive
Suite 1201
Stanford, CA 94305

Dear Ms. Pallos:

Thank you for your letter regarding the upcoming
event. I am in complete agreement with you that the
number of persons attending must be limited to 350.
In addition, your idea of having this event catered
sounds fantastic.

Moving to a different subject, I noticed that the
letter you wrote me was typed using a typewriter.
(You certainly do use enough correction fluid!) With
the number of letters you write, you really should
consider purchasing a microcomputer and word
processing software program.

If you are interested, come over to my office and I
will show you some word processing fundamentals. We
could even use my computer to design and print the
invitations for the event!

Best regards,

your name

a. Insert the following text between the second and third paragraphs:

    Specifically, word processing software makes
    it easier to change a document by allowing
    you to:

    1.   Insert text
    2.   Move text
    3.   Copy text
    4.   Delete text

    b. In the first line of the last paragraph, delete the words "If you are interested," and start the sentence with "You should."

    c. In the second paragraph, replace the phrase "correction fluid" with "whiteout."

    d. Save the document back to the Advantage Diskette as NEWLET.

    e. Print the document.

    f. Quit Write.

2. In this exercise, create the picture appearing in Figure 4.11 using the Paintbrush drawing program. When you are finished, save the image as BARGRAPH onto the Advantage Diskette and then send the picture to the printer.

Figure 4.11

The BARGRAPH drawing in Paintbrush

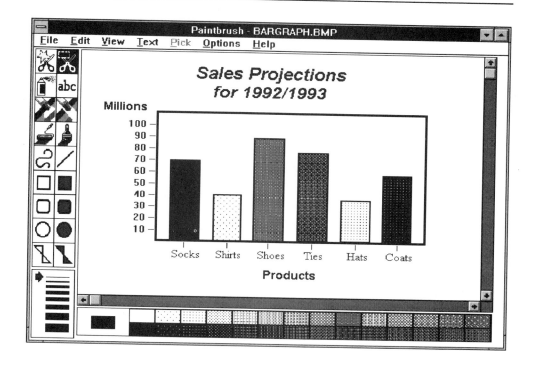

3. Using Cardfile, create and save a file on the Advantage Diskette called CLIENTS that contains the information provided on the next page. Each row in the table should be placed onto a separate card.

    a. Sort the cards according to the client's surname. (Hint: A card file is sorted by the information appearing in the index line.)

    b. Print two reports: a summary list and the complete card information.

Given	Surname	Address	City	State	Zip
Elliot	Lepinski	898 Burrard Avenue	Louisville	KY	40205
Red	Robinson	235 Johnson Street	Washington	DC	20052
Elaine	Maynard	1005 West 9th Street, #705	Baton Rouge	LA	70803
Ranjitt	Singh	1227 E. Cordova Avenue	Tacoma	WA	98416
William	Delaney	36 Primore Road	Wichita	KS	67208
Francisco	Ortez	875 Broadway	Albuquerque	NM	87131
Alice	Chan	29 Redmond Road	San Francisco	CA	92182
Jessica	Thomas	909 West 18th Street, #12	Brooklyn	NY	11225
Jimmy	Kazo	888 East 8th Avenue	Billings	MT	59101
Kelly	Judson	1984 Orwell Road	Tacoma	WA	98405
Paul	Mang	12555 Horseshoe Way	Washington	DC	20055
Wanda	Roo	Building C, 10 Main St.	Brooklyn	NY	11230

SESSION 5

WINDOWS 3.1:
INCREASING YOUR
PRODUCTIVITY

Since the introduction of the IBM PC in the early 1980s, computers have heralded the promise of greater efficiency and productivity. With Microsoft Windows, the promise approaches reality. For most people, the graphical interface and consistency among Windows applications makes learning computers easier and less frustrating. However, there are always some individuals who prefer the challenge of tinkering under the hood. This session introduces you to the tools and concepts that make Windows so powerful.

PREVIEW

When you have completed this session, you will be able to:

Associate data files to application program files.

•

Explain the advantages of multitasking.

•

Use Task Manager to switch among running applications.

•

Explain the process of pasting, linking, and embedding data.

•

Create macros using the Recorder accessory program.

•

Discuss memory management.

•

Run DOS applications under Microsoft Windows.

WHY IS THIS SESSION IMPORTANT?

This session strays somewhat from the task-oriented approach of previous sessions. Rather than performing hands-on examples for each topic, this session explores some of the concepts behind Microsoft Windows. The initial sections illustrate the capabilities of multitasking using Task Manager. Although you only multitask the Windows accessory programs in this guide, you can apply these principles to your regular applications, such as Word for Windows, WordPerfect for Windows, Excel for Windows, or Lotus for Windows. Windows is an exceptional task switcher that allows you to load commonly used programs into memory and then switch among them quickly and easily.

Windows increases your productivity. We have promised this before, but you will see it demonstrated in this session. For example, the Sharing Data section explains the concepts of pasting, linking, and embedding information. Read this section carefully! Understanding the process of sharing information in Windows enables you to vault up the productivity curve.

Another important topic for increasing your productivity is macros. The Recorder accessory program enables you to record keystrokes and mouse actions for later playback. With Recorder, you automate many routine tasks in Windows by assigning them to macros. The latter half of this session explores memory management. Understanding memory allocation enables you to fine-tune Windows to optimize its performance. This session concludes with a discussion on running DOS applications under Windows. With this capability, you may never use the DOS prompt again.

Before proceeding, make sure the following are true:

1. You have turned on your computer system and loaded Windows 3.1.
2. The Program Manager window appears on the screen.
3. Your Advantage Diskette is inserted into drive A:. You will work with files on the diskette that have been created for you. (Note: The Advantage Diskette can be duplicated by copying all of the files from your instructor's Master Advantage Diskette.)

FILE ASSOCIATION

Windows provides three ways to start application software programs. Most commonly, you create a program item icon for an application and place it into a group window. To start the application, you double-click the program icon. A second method for starting applications is to choose the File, Run command from the Program Manager window and then enter the program's filename in the dialog box. You can also double-click a program file in the directory contents pane of File Manager. To use the Run command or File Manager, you must enter or select a program filename recognized by Windows, which includes files with the extension BAT (batch file), COM (command file), EXE (executable file), or PIF (program information file).

Using File Manager, you can teach Windows a few shortcuts by associating data files with program files. When you double-click an associated data file (also called a document file), Windows automatically loads the document and the application you used to create it. For example, files with the extension XLS are associated with the Microsoft Excel program file, EXCEL.EXE. Files with the extensions WRI and DOC are associated with Windows Write and Microsoft Word program files, respectively. To associate a data file, you select the file in the directory contents pane and then issue the File, Associate command from the menu.

Perform the following steps.

1. Load File Manager from the Main group window.

2. To display the files for drive A:, do the following:
   PRESS: Ctrl+a

3. Notice the different icons for program files (⬜), document files (📄), and data files (🗋). To associate the PHONES.DAT data file with the PHONES.EXE program file, you must first select the PHONES.DAT file in the directory contents pane:
   SELECT: PHONES.DAT data file

4. To associate the data file:
   CHOOSE: File, Associate
   The Associate dialog box appears, as displayed in Figure 5.1.

Figure 5.1

The Associate
dialog box

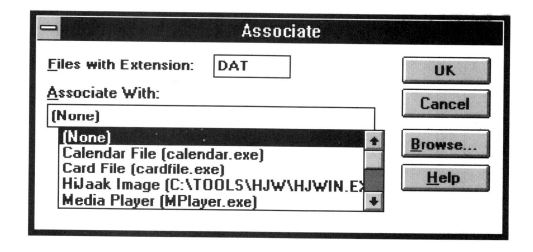

5. Because Windows does not recognize the extension DAT, there is no program file shown in the Associate With list box. To select the PHONES.EXE program file:
   SELECT: Browse command button

6. In the Browse dialog box:
   SELECT: PHONES.EXE from the list box
   PRESS: (Enter) or CLICK: OK

7. When you return to the Associate dialog box:
   PRESS: (Enter) or CLICK: OK
   Notice that the PHONES.DAT file has a document file icon.

8. To launch the PHONES application, you can now double-click on *any* file that has the extension DAT. When you associate a file, you are associating an extension with an application program, not just a single file. To start the PHONES program:
   DOUBLE-CLICK: PHONES.DAT

9. After the PHONES application loads, exit the program:
   PRESS: (F10)

10. Exit File Manager:
    CHOOSE: File, Exit

Quick Reference
*Associating a
Data File*
1. In File Manager, select a data file from the directory contents pane.
2. To associate the data file with an application program file, choose File, Associate from the menu.
3. Select the application from the list box or use the Browse command button to specify an unlisted program file.
4. Press (Enter) or click on OK.

MULTITASKING

With Windows multitasking capabilities, you can execute multiple application programs concurrently. Multitasking distributes the computer's processing time among running applications in memory. As you will see in this section, the advantages of multitasking are numerous. For example, you can load several programs into memory without having to exit the current program, and switch among them easily. Besides saving you time, multitasking facilitates the exchange of data between application programs.

TASK MANAGER

Multitasking in Windows is controlled using Task Manager. Task Manager enables you to list running applications, move among them, and close applications. To display Task Manager, press (Ctrl)+(Esc) or double-click on an empty area of the Desktop.

To move quickly among running applications, you can bypass Task Manager altogether by holding down the (Alt) key while you press (Tab). With each press of the (Tab) key, the name of a running application appears on a message board in the middle of the screen. When the name of the desired application appears, you release the (Alt) key to move to that application.

Perform the following steps to practice switching among applications.

1. Load Write from the Accessories group and minimize it to an icon.

2. Load Paintbrush from the Accessories group and minimize it to an icon.

3. Load Calculator from the Accessories group and minimize it to an icon.

4. Load Clock from the Accessories group and minimize it to an icon. (<u>Note</u>: The Clock program may already be minimized on the Desktop. If so, you can proceed to the next step.)

5. Minimize the Program Manager window.
   As demonstrated, minimizing an application program places its icon along the bottom row of the Desktop, but does not end the program.

6. To display Task Manager:
   DOUBLE-CLICK: an empty area on the Desktop

7. To switch to Write, position the mouse pointer over Write in the list box and then do the following:
   CLICK: left mouse button once

8 SELECT: Switch To command button
   The Write window appears on the Desktop.

9. To use the Windows Calculator:
   PRESS: Ctrl+Esc
   DOUBLE-CLICK: Calculator in the list box

10. To switch to Clock without using Task Manager:
    PRESS: Alt and hold it down
    PRESS: Tab several times to cycle through the running applications

11. Release the Alt key when Clock appears in the message board.

12. To close Paintbrush:
    PRESS: Ctrl+Esc
    SELECT: Paintbrush in the list box
    SELECT: End Task command button

Quick Reference
Using Task
Manager

- To display Task Manager, double-click an empty area on the Desktop or press Ctrl+Esc.
- To move to an application, highlight an application in the list box and then press Enter or select the Switch To command button. You can also double-click an application name in the list box.
- To close an application, highlight an application in the list box and then select the End Task command button.

SOLVING CONFLICTS

When you work with several applications at once, the probability of experiencing problems greatly increases. Although most Windows programs work well in a multitasking environment, some applications respond poorly when they must share system resources. In Windows 3.0, ill-behaved applications often produced UAEs or Unrecoverable Application Errors that mysteriously locked the computer. Windows 3.1 improves error detection, tracking, and resolution with a diagnostic tool called Dr. Watson and a feature called Application Reboot.

The Dr. Watson utility diagnoses application errors and records important system information when an error occurs. This information is stored in a file called DRWATSON.LOG and may be used by the Microsoft technical support team to help solve your problems. To use Dr. Watson, you load the program from the Accessories group window. If the icon does not appear in the group, create a new program item and specify DRWATSON.EXE on the command line. Because Dr. Watson must be running in memory at the time an error occurs, you may want to place a copy of the program item in the StartUp group.

The Application Reboot feature enables you to close a single application that freezes or locks the computer. Without Application Reboot, you would have to reboot the entire computer when a program failed to respond to the keyboard or a mouse. After performing a successful Application Reboot to unlock an application, you should save your documents in the other running applications and then restart Windows. To perform an Application Reboot, you hold down Ctrl+Alt and then tap the Delete key. Perform this key combination *only* when your computer is locked and you cannot exit a program.

SHARING DATA

Windows enables you to easily exchange information among different applications. Although the most common example involves placing numbers from a worksheet into a word processing document, you can also transfer graphics and sound recordings. A document that contains data from another application is called a **compound document** or a destination document. The application that accepts data into a compound document is called the **client application**. The document in which the data was first composed, before being transferred to a compound document, is called a

source document. The application that you use to create the source document is called the **server application**.

Windows provides three primary methods for sharing information: **pasting**, **linking**, and **embedding**. Regardless of the method, the process is very similar to a regular cut or copy and paste procedure. For example, to copy numbers from a worksheet into a document, you select the numbers and then issue the <u>E</u>dit, <u>C</u>opy command to transfer them to the Clipboard. After moving to the word processing application using Task Manager or [Alt]+[Tab], you issue the <u>E</u>dit, <u>P</u>aste command to place a copy of the Clipboard data into the document. The <u>E</u>dit, Paste <u>L</u>ink or <u>E</u>dit, Paste <u>S</u>pecial commands allow you to link the file or embed an object into the document, as explained in the next few sections.

USING THE CLIPBOARD

When you cut or copy information from a document, Windows places the information in an area of memory called the Clipboard. You can paste the contents of the Clipboard to another location in the same application or to another application. The pasted information remains static and is not updated when you change the original or source document. When you paste information, you are not supplying a link between applications or document files; you are simply placing a snapshot of information into the destination document. Pasting is used when you need to perform a one-time exchange of information.

To update the pasted data in the destination document, you must repeat the process of copying from the source document. The information resides on the Clipboard until it is cleared or another piece of information is cut or copied. You can use the Clipboard Viewer program from the Main group window to view the contents of the Clipboard.

DYNAMIC DATA EXCHANGE (DDE)

In version 3.0, Windows introduced the Dynamic Data Exchange (DDE) protocol that allows application software programs to dynamically share information. Rather than using the static pasting of <u>E</u>dit, <u>P</u>aste, you can use the <u>E</u>dit, Paste <u>L</u>ink or <u>E</u>dit, Paste <u>S</u>pecial commands to establish a link between the source and compound documents. When you make changes in the source document (using the server application), the information in the linked compound document (client application) is automatically updated.

You link files when you need information from a source document to be used in multiple compound documents. For example, you may have a monthly sales forecast that you need included in several related reports. In this case, linking the compound report documents to the one source document is the most efficient method for automatically updating the reports when the forecast changes. As you may expect, linking is very useful for sharing information over networks. People working together on projects can easily share information by simply linking their files to their team members' documents.

OBJECT LINKING AND EMBEDDING (OLE)

Object Linking and Embedding (OLE) is designed into Windows applications to facilitate sharing and manipulating information. Embedding information involves inserting an object into a compound document (client application) from a source document (server application). Unlike a link between files, an embedded object retains a link to the server application but not to the source document. By double-clicking on the object in the compound document, you can load the server application, make and save changes, and automatically update the object without leaving the compound document. Because an OLE object is not linked to an external file, you have everything contained in a single document.

As the latest and greatest in compound document technology, OLE is now supported by almost every current version of Windows software, including some Windows accessories. For example, Paintbrush and Sound Recorder are OLE server applications, while Write and Cardfile are OLE client applications.

COPYING AND PASTING INFORMATION

In this section, you copy and paste information among applications. Using information from the previous three sections on pasting, linking, and embedding, you perform a hands-on example that demonstrates these powerful features.

Perform the following steps.

1. Ensure that Program Manager appears on the screen. If it is minimized, double-click the Program Manager icon at the bottom of the Desktop.

2. To display the currently running applications, call up Task Manager:
PRESS: [Ctrl]+[Esc]

3. Make sure that Write and Calculator appear in the task list. If not, do the following:
PRESS: [Esc] to remove Task Manager from the Desktop
SELECT: Accessories group window in Program Manager
DOUBLE-CLICK: Write program icon
SELECT: Accessories group window in Program Manager
DOUBLE-CLICK: Calculator program icon

4. Make Write the active application window:
PRESS: [Ctrl]+[Esc]
DOUBLE-CLICK: Write option in the task list

5. In Write, add three blank lines at the top of the document:
PRESS: [Enter] three times

6. Enter the following information:
TYPE: JANUARY
PRESS: [Enter] twice
TYPE: Rent
PRESS: [Tab]
TYPE: $852
PRESS: [Enter]
TYPE: Food
PRESS: [Tab]
TYPE: $227
PRESS: [Enter]
TYPE: Gas
PRESS: [Tab]
TYPE: $119
PRESS: [Enter] twice
TYPE: Total
PRESS: [Tab]
TYPE: $

7. Use the Windows Calculator program to sum the numbers:
PRESS: [Ctrl]+[Esc]
DOUBLE-CLICK: Calculator
The Calculator window becomes active.

8. To sum the three numbers:
   TYPE: 852+227+119
   TYPE: =
   The result, 1198, appears in the Calculator window. Your screen should now appear similar to Figure 5.2.

Figure 5.2

Working with
multiple
applications

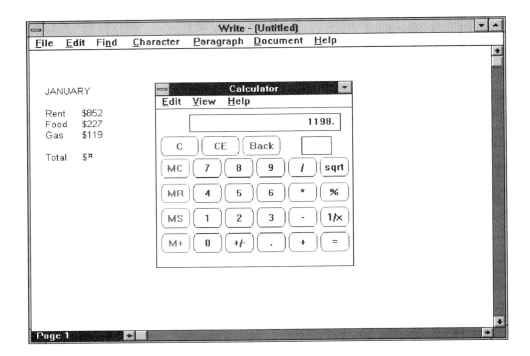

9. To copy the result from Calculator:
   CHOOSE: Edit, Copy from the Calculator Menu bar

10. After copying the result to the Clipboard, move to the Write document:
    CLICK: *anywhere in the Write application window*

11. To paste the result of the calculation, move the cursor to the Total line and then do the following:
    CHOOSE: Edit, Paste from the Write Menu bar

12. Move to the top of the document:
    PRESS: Ctrl+Home

13. Select the entire document:
    PRESS: Shift and hold it down
    PRESS: Ctrl+End

14. To copy the selected area:
     CHOOSE: Edit, Copy
     The information is placed on the Clipboard.

15. To view the information on the Clipboard:
     PRESS: [Alt] and hold it down
     PRESS: [Tab] until the Program Manager appears

16. Release the [Alt] key to move to the Program Manager window.

17. To start the Clipboard Viewer:
     SELECT: Main group window
     DOUBLE-CLICK: Clipboard Viewer program icon
     Notice that the contents of the Write document are displayed in the
     Clipboard Viewer's window.

18. Close the Clipboard Viewer:
     CHOOSE: File, Exit

19. Select and close the Calculator application window.

20. Select and close the Write application window without saving the
     document.

21. Select and close all other application windows, except for Program
     Manager. (Hint: Using the Task Manager, highlight a task and select
     the End Task command button. Remember, you cannot end Program
     Manager without quitting Windows.)

....

Quick Reference   • To copy information, choose Edit, Copy.
Copying and   • To move information, choose Edit, Cut.
Pasting Information • To paste information, choose Edit, Paste.
                      • To link or embed information, choose Edit, Paste Link or Edit, Paste
                         Special once the information has been placed on the Clipboard.

....

Using Object Packager

The Object Packager enables you to create objects to embed into client applications that support OLE. Aside from specifying the programs to be included in the package, you can select an icon and title for the object. For example, you could create an object that launches the Windows Calculator and then paste that object into a frequently used worksheet document. To use Calculator in the worksheet, you would simply double-click on the object's icon.

To load Object Packager, open the Accessories group window and double-click the Object Packager program icon. Two panes appear in the Object Packager application window: the Content pane and the Appearance pane. In the Content pane, you select Edit, Command Line from the menu to specify a program to include in the package. When finished entering the program's name, click the Appearance pane to specify an icon. Select the Insert Icon command button, highlight an appropriate icon, and press (Enter) or click on OK. To specify a name for the icon, choose Edit, Label from the menu and then press (Enter). To insert the object into a document, choose Edit, Copy Package from the menu to place it on the Clipboard.

Perform the following steps.

1. Ensure that Program Manager appears on the screen.

2. To load Object Packager:
   SELECT: Accessories group
   DOUBLE-CLICK: Object Packager program icon

3. Select the Content window:
   CLICK: Content window

4. To create a package for a program file:
   CHOOSE: Edit, Command Line

5. Create a package for the Calculator:
   TYPE: calc.exe
   PRESS: (Enter) or CLICK: OK

6. Select the Appearance window:
   CLICK: Appearance window

7. To select an icon for the new package:
   SELECT: Insert Icon command button
   SELECT: *any icon from the horizontal scroll list*
   PRESS: (Enter) or CLICK: OK

8. To name the object package:
   CHOOSE: Edit, Label
   TYPE: Quick Calc
   PRESS: (Enter) or CLICK: OK
   Your screen should now appear similar to Figure 5.3.

Figure 5.3

The Object
Packager dialog
box

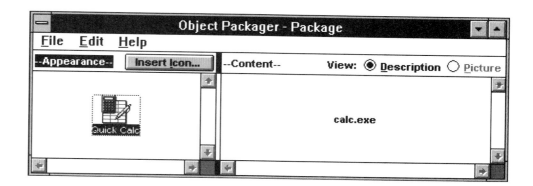

9. To copy the package to the Clipboard:
   CHOOSE: Edit, Copy Package

10. SELECT: Accessories group window in Program Manager

11. DOUBLE-CLICK: Write
    An empty document appears.

12. To insert the Quick Calc object package as an embedded object:
    CHOOSE: Edit, Paste Special from the menu
    CHOOSE: Paste command button
    The icon appears in the document.

13. To quickly load Calculator:
    DOUBLE-CLICK: Quick Calc icon

14. Close the Calculator window:
    DOUBLE-CLICK: Control menu for the Calculator window

15. Exit Write and do not save the changes. If prompted to update the embedded object, select No.

Quick Reference
Creating an Object Package

1. Open the Accessories group and double-click on the Object Packager program icon.
2. To specify a program for the package, choose Edit, Command Line.
3. Type the name of the program and press (Enter) or click on OK.
4. Select the Appearance window.
5. To specify an icon for the object package, select the Insert Icon command button.
6. Select an icon and then press (Enter) or click on OK.
7. To copy the package for embedding into a document, choose the Edit, Copy Package command from the menu.

USING RECORDER

Using the Windows Recorder, you create macros to automate commands and procedures. Macros not only save you time, they improve the consistency and reliability of routine activities. A **macro** is a collection of keystrokes and mouse operations that have been recorded and stored in a disk file. Using a macro involves pressing as few as two keys to execute the recorded keystrokes, whereas performing the same procedure without a macro usually involves pressing many keys. This section explains how to create and play back macros.

RECORDING A MACRO

You create a macro by recording keystrokes and mouse operations using Recorder. To load Recorder, select the Accessories group window and then double-click the Recorder program icon. When ready to begin recording, you generally perform the following steps:

a. Move to the application where you will record and play the macro.
b. Make Recorder the active application window.
c. CHOOSE: Macro, Record from the Recorder menu
d. Specify the macro name and shortcut key.
e. PRESS: (Enter) or CLICK: Start
f. Perform the keystrokes and mouse operations to be recorded.

   g. When finished recording, press [Ctrl]+[Break].

   h. Choose whether to save the macro, resume recording, or cancel recording.

   i. PRESS: [Enter] or CLICK: OK

Perform the following steps to record a macro that automatically inserts a closing statement for letters created in the Write word processing program.

1. Close all application windows, except for Program Manager.

2. To load Recorder:
   SELECT: Accessories group
   DOUBLE-CLICK: Recorder program icon

3. Return to the Program Manager:
   PRESS: [Ctrl]+[Esc]
   DOUBLE-CLICK: Program Manager in the task list

4. To load Write:
   SELECT: Accessories group
   DOUBLE-CLICK: Write program icon

5. Make the Recorder application window active:
   PRESS: [Ctrl]+[Esc]
   DOUBLE-CLICK: Recorder

6. To record keystrokes for the macro:
   CHOOSE: Macro, Record
   The Record Macro dialog box appears, as shown in Figure 5.4.

Figure 5.4

Record Macro
dialog box

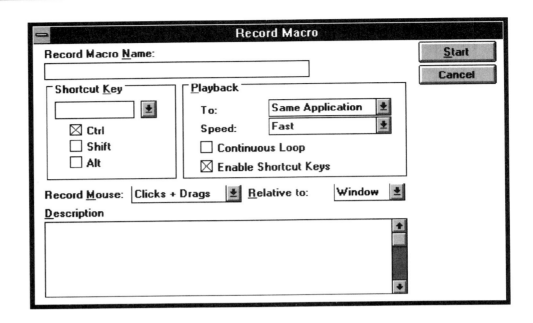

7. To name the macro:
    TYPE: closing
    PRESS: [Tab]

8. To assign a shortcut key for executing the macro:
    TYPE: s
    PRESS: [Enter] or CLICK: Start
    The Recorder window reduces to a flashing icon at the bottom of the
    Desktop.

    CAUTION: Some shortcut key combinations are used commonly in
    Windows applications (for example, [Ctrl]+c for copying, [Ctrl]+x for
    cutting, and [Ctrl]+v for pasting). Do not assign a shortcut key that
    conflicts with these standard key combinations. For this example, you
    assign an s for *signature*, rather than c for *closing*.

9. In the Write document, enter the following:
    TYPE: Sincerely yours,
    PRESS: [Enter] four times
    TYPE: *your name*
    PRESS: [Enter]
    TYPE: President

10. To stop the Recorder:
    PRESS: [Ctrl]+[Break]

11. The resulting dialog box asks whether to save, resume, or cancel the macro. For this example, save the macro:
    SELECT: Save Macro
    PRESS: [Enter] or CLICK: OK

12. To save the macro to the disk, make Recorder active:
    PRESS: [Ctrl]+[Esc]
    DOUBLE-CLICK: Recorder
    Notice that the closing macro appears in the work area.

13. CHOOSE: File, Save As
    TYPE: a:\macros
    PRESS: [Enter]
    Recorder automatically adds an extension of REC to the file name.

14. Minimize the Recorder application window.

15. Request a new document in the Write application window:
    CHOOSE: File, New
    SELECT: No when asked to save the existing file

16. To run the macro using the shortcut key:
    PRESS: [Ctrl]+s
    The closing is automatically inserted into the document.

Quick Reference
Recording a Macro

1. Open the Accessories group and double-click on the Recorder program item icon.
2. To record a macro, choose Macro, Record from the menu.
3. Name the macro and assign it a shortcut key combination.
4. Press [Enter] or click on the Start command button.
5. Perform the keystrokes as usual.
6. Press [Ctrl]+[Break] to save, resume, or cancel the recording.

PLAYING BACK A MACRO

There are two primary methods for playing back a macro. As seen in the previous section, you can execute a macro by pressing its [Ctrl]+letter combination. However, there may be times when you forget the key combination. For these cases, Recorder provides a list of the macros in the application window. You can highlight the desired macro in the list and choose Macro, Run, or simply double-click the macro.

Perform the following steps.

1. In continuation from the last section, you will insert another copy of the closing statement in the current document. To begin, enter two blank lines in the Write document:
   PRESS: (Enter) twice

2. To perform the closing macro from the Recorder application window:
   PRESS: (Ctrl)+(Esc)
   DOUBLE-CLICK: Recorder

3. Since there is only one macro in the list, the closing macro is automatically highlighted. To run the macro:
   CHOOSE: Macro, Run
   The macro performs the keystrokes from the last known cursor position in the Write document. (Note: You can also double-click the macro name in the Recorder application window.)

....

Quick Reference   To play back a macro:
Playing Back a   PRESS: the assigned shortcut key, or
Macro   CHOOSE: Macro, Run from the Recorder's pull-down menu

....

MEMORY MANAGEMENT

With a basic understanding of hardware and software interdependencies, you can optimize the performance of Windows on your computer. In addition to sophisticated multitasking capabilities, Windows provides enhanced **memory management**. This section explains the different types of memory.

TYPES OF MEMORY

There are two primary types of memory, ROM and RAM. ROM is read-only memory and contains the instructions for the basic input and output operations of the computer. These instructions are permanently encoded onto special chips. RAM, or random-access memory, is volatile memory and provides the interactive work area for your programs and data. RAM is divided into conventional, extended, and expanded memory.

Conventional memory is the area from 0 KB to 640 KB in RAM. This memory area provides the workspace for the majority of your programs and data. Because 640 KB is a fundamental DOS limitation, you run out of memory if you consume all the conventional memory—no matter how much extended or expanded memory is available. The memory area between 640 KB and 1 MB is called the upper memory area or reserved memory. This area is reserved for managing various hardware devices, such as a graphics adapter.

Extended memory (XMS) exists above the 1 MB address space. A memory manager, such as HIMEM.SYS, is required to access extended memory. The first 64 KB block of extended memory is called the High Memory Area (HMA). DOS 5.0 takes advantage of computers with extended memory by loading some operating system instructions into the HMA. This frees up space in conventional memory for your programs and data. If you are serious about using Windows, you should upgrade to DOS 5.0 if you have not done so already.

Expanded memory (EMS) usually refers to a memory board that you add to your computer. However, you can use extended memory to emulate expanded memory with the proper software. Although once popular, expanded memory is now used by relatively few programs.

OPTIMIZING WINDOWS

A general rule of thumb for enhancing Windows' performance is to add more memory (RAM). With sufficient memory and an 80386 computer, you can efficiently perform multitasking of several applications. In addition to reducing the need for disk swapping, you can increase the speed of disk operations using a **disk cache** utility program (discussed in the Speeding Up Windows section). On the other hand, you are still limited by the 640 KB DOS barrier for applications regardless of the amount of RAM in your computer. This shortcoming of DOS has spawned the latest interest in Windows NT and OS/2 operating systems, which both surpass this ridiculous barrier.

SPEEDING UP WINDOWS

When you first load Windows, it examines your computer equipment and loads using one of two modes: standard or 386 enhanced. If you use an 80286 computer, Windows runs in standard mode which allows access to 16 MB of extended memory and multitasking of Windows applications. If you use an 80386 computer with 2 MB of RAM or higher, Windows runs in 386 enhanced mode which provides access to virtual memory and allows you to multitask both Windows and DOS applications.

VIRTUAL MEMORY

To run several applications at once in 386 enhanced mode, you can use a swap file to increase the memory available to applications. A swap file provides virtual memory by using the hard disk to simulate RAM. When an application requests memory, Windows allocates physical RAM first and then uses a disk swap file. In Windows 386 enhanced mode, you can specify a permanent or a temporary swap file. Although a permanent swap file is generally faster, it consumes disk space even when you are not using Windows. A temporary swap file grows and shrinks as needed, and is deleted when you exit Windows. Because accessing the disk is 50 times slower than accessing RAM, you should increase your computer's memory if you notice a degradation in speed due to disk swapping.

To change your swap file settings, double-click the 386 Enhanced program icon in the Control Panel dialog box. Select the Virtual Memory command button to display the current settings and then choose the Change>> button to modify the swap file. Before enabling a permanent swap file, you should defragment your disk to ensure that there is a large area of contiguous storage available. A permanent swap file must be stored in a contiguous area of your hard disk and can be a maximum of three times the size of your physical RAM. A swap file is stored on the disk in a file called WIN386.SWP; do not delete or attempt to modify this file during a Windows session.

DISK CACHES

The SmartDrive disk-caching program that is provided with Windows 3.1 increases performance by saving frequently accessed information from your hard disk in extended memory. The SmartDrive method of buffering hard disk activity is called read-ahead and write-behind disk caching. Read-ahead caching stores data that is read from the hard disk in memory, so that Windows does not need to go back to the hard disk the next time you need the data. Write-behind caching delays writing data to the disk, so that you do not experience a lag due to constant disk writing. The optimum SmartDrive cache depends on your system configuration and available RAM.

RUNNING DOS APPLICATIONS

You can launch DOS applications from Program Manager or File Manager. In order to optimize the performance of DOS applications, Windows provides PIF (Program Information File) files that contain special configuration options for setting graphics and memory usage. You use the PIF Editor (Figure 5.5), accessible from the Main group, to modify these settings or create your own PIF files. If you do not specify a PIF file for a DOS application, Windows uses a standard PIF file with default settings.

Figure 5.5

The PIF Editor dialog box

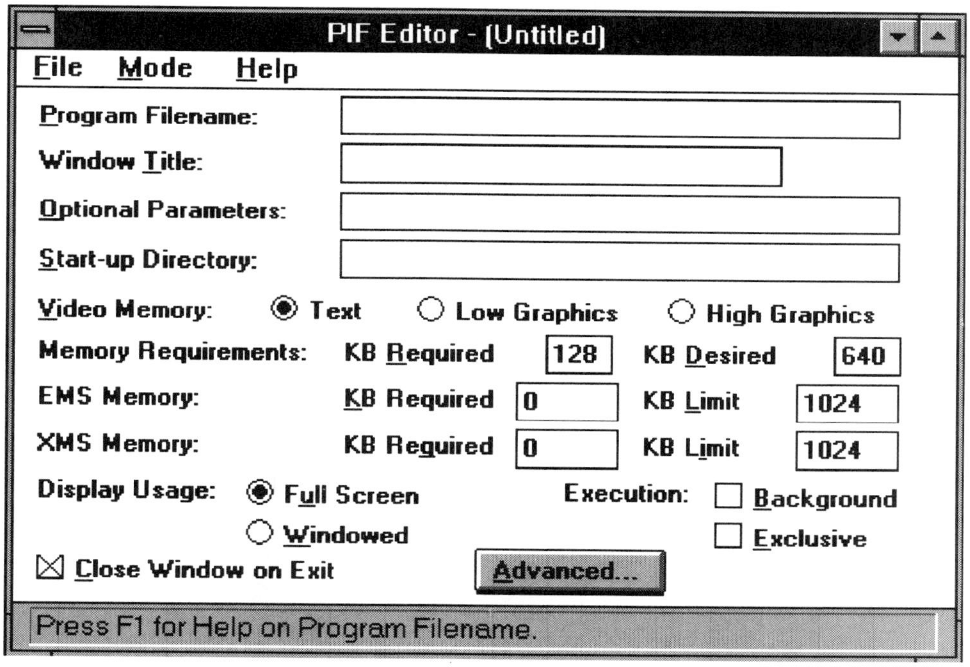

Windows 3.1 also provides mouse support for mouse-capable DOS applications, font control to adjust the size of a windowed application, and cut, copy, and paste capabilities. To quickly switch between a full-screen and windowed display of a DOS application, press (Alt)+(Enter).

CHANGING FONTS

You can change the font size appearing in a windowed DOS application by choosing the Fonts command from the Control menu. When you highlight a font, a preview appears in the Window Preview box and the Selected Font box. These preview boxes help you determine how a font affects the readability of a window. Select the desired font size from the Font list box and press (Enter) or click on OK.

Perform the following steps.

1. Close all application windows, except for Program Manager.

2. To load File Manager and select drive A:, do the following:
    SELECT: Main group
    DOUBLE-CLICK: File Manager program icon
    PRESS: (Ctrl)+a

3. To run the PHONES application on the Advantage Diskette:
    CHOOSE: File, Run
    TYPE: phones.exe
    PRESS: (Enter) or CLICK: OK
    The standard PIF file for DOS applications specifies a full-screen session in Windows.

4. After the application loads, change the session from a full screen to a window:
    PRESS: (Alt)+(Enter)

5. To change the font for the PHONES application window:
    CHOOSE: Fonts from the Control menu
    The Fonts dialog box appears on the screen, as shown in Figure 5.6.

Figure 5.6

The Fonts dialog
box for a DOS
application

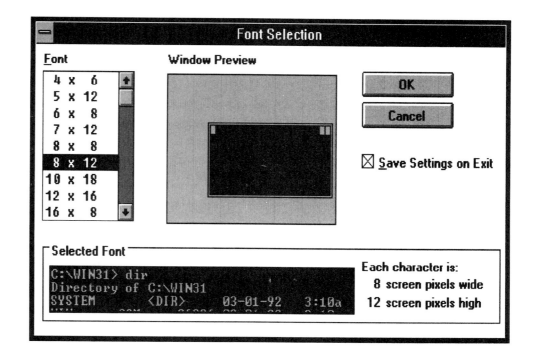

6. SELECT: 7 × 12 option from the list box
   PRESS: Enter or CLICK: OK

7. To quit the PHONES application:
   PRESS: F10

8. Close the File Manager application window.

Quick Reference
Running DOS
Applications

• To change a DOS session from a full screen to a window, press Alt+Enter.
• To change the font size displayed in a DOS window, choose the Fonts command from the Control menu.

SUMMARY

This session introduced several topics for increasing your productivity and optimizing Windows performance. To begin the session, you used the file association feature in File Manager to launch a document with its application. After seeing the advantages of multitasking, you used Task Manager to switch among several Windows accessory programs that were running concurrently. Three methods for sharing data were also discussed including pasting (Clipboard), linking (DDE), and embedding (OLE).

Two accessory programs, Object Packager and Recorder, were demonstrated in this session. Object Packager creates objects out of programs and files that can be embedded into compound documents. Recorder enables you to record keystrokes and mouse operations to automate routine tasks. This session also explored memory management and discussed a few topics for enhancing Windows. A brief section on running non-Windows applications concluded the session.

Many of the commands and procedures introduced in this session appear in the Command Summary (Table 5.1).

Table 5.1	*Command*	*Description*
Command Summary	File, Run	In File Manager and Program Manager, allows you to launch application programs
	File, Associate	In File Manager, creates a document file by associating a data file with a program file
	Edit, Copy	Copies selected information to the Clipboard
	Edit, Cut	Moves selected information from a document to the Clipboard
	Edit, Paste	Pastes information from the Clipboard
	Edit, Paste Link	Pastes information from the Clipboard and links the compound document to the source document (DDE)
	Edit, Paste Special	Pastes information from the Clipboard and links the compound document to the server application (OLE)

Table 5.1	*Command*	*Description*
Continued	<u>E</u>dit, Co<u>mm</u>and Line	In Object Packager, specifies a program to include in an object
	<u>E</u>dit, La<u>b</u>el	In Object Packager, assigns a name to an object icon
	<u>E</u>dit, Copy Pac<u>k</u>age	In Object Packager, copies a package to the Clipboard
	<u>M</u>acro, Re<u>c</u>ord	In Recorder, turns on the keystroke and mouse recorder
	<u>M</u>acro, <u>R</u>un	In Recorder, runs the highlighted macro
Useful Keystrokes	Ctrl+Esc	Displays Task Manager
	Alt+Tab	Cycles through the running application programs
	Alt+Enter	Changes a DOS session from a full screen to a window

KEY TERMS

client application   An application that accepts data into a compound document.

compound document   A document that contains data from another application.

conventional memory   The area from 0 KB to 640 KB in RAM memory.

disk cache   An area in memory that is used to store information read from the disk; speeds up disk operations.

embedding   A way of sharing and exchanging information; refers to the process of inserting an object into a compound document that is linked to the server application.

expanded memory   Additional memory, usually provided by an add-in memory board; extended memory can emulate expanded memory.

extended memory   The area above 1 MB in RAM memory.

linking   A way of sharing and exchanging information; refers to the process of copying information from a source document into a compound document and establishing a dynamic link between the two.

macro   A collection of recorded keystrokes and mouse actions that automates routine tasks.

memory management   The process by which the operating system allows applications to access memory.

pasting   A way of sharing and exchanging information; refers to the process of copying static information from a source document into a destination document without linking the two documents.

server application   An application that you use to create a source document.

source document   The original document in which information is created for transfer to a compound document.

EXERCISES

SHORT ANSWER

1. Why would you want to associate a data file with a program file?
2. What are the four types of program files recognized by Windows?
3. What is multitasking?
4. What Windows feature would you use if your keyboard didn't respond?
5. Describe the process of pasting information using the Clipboard.
6. Describe the process of linking information using Dynamic Data Exchange (DDE).
7. Describe the process of embedding an object using Object Linking and Embedding (OLE).
8. In this session, you created a macro to automate the signing of a closing statement on a letter. Name another routine task that you could automate with a macro.
9. What is the purpose of a swap file?
10. What is SmartDrive?

HANDS-ON

(Note: In the following exercises, you perform Windows commands using files located on the Advantage Diskette.)

1. This exercise demonstrates Windows multitasking capabilities and lets you practice positioning and moving among running applications.
   a. Ensure that the Program Manager application window appears on the Desktop.
   b. Load Notepad from the Accessories group window.
   c. Return to Program Manager using [Alt]+[Tab].
   d. Load Paintbrush from the Accessories group window.
   e. Return to Program Manager using [Alt]+[Tab].
   f. Load Write from the Accessories group window.
   g. Return to Program Manager using [Alt]+[Tab].
   h. Load Clipboard Viewer from the Main group window.
   i. Return to Program Manager using [Alt]+[Tab].
   j. Minimize the Program Manager application window.
   k. Call up the Windows Task Manager:
      PRESS: [Ctrl]+[Esc]
   l. You should have the following programs displayed in the task list: Clipboard Viewer, Write, Paintbrush, Notepad, and Program Manager. If you have any other applications, highlight the application name in the task list and then select the End Task command button.
   m. To organize the running applications on the Desktop, select the Cascade command button in Task Manager. Your screen should appear similar to Figure 5.7.

Figure 5.7

Cascading open
application
programs

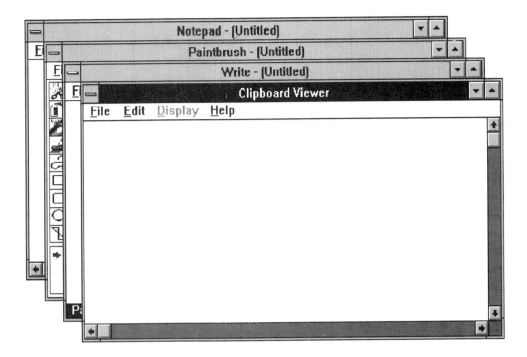

n. To tile the running applications on the Desktop, select the Tile
    command button in Task Manager:
    PRESS: Ctrl+Esc
    SELECT: Tile command button
o. After tiling the running application windows, you can easily move
    among them using the mouse:
    CLICK: Write window
    CLICK: Notepad window
    Watch the Title bars of the application windows to see which
    window is active.
p. To switch to the next application in the task list using the keyboard:
    PRESS: Alt and hold it down
    PRESS: Tab until the name of the desired application appears
    Release the Alt key.
q. Continue pressing Alt+Tab to move to each application. Select
    Notepad before proceeding to the next exercise.

2. This exercise continues the example of multitasking introduced in the
    first exercise. In the following steps, you copy information among the
    applications.
    a. In the Notepad window, enter the following information:
        TYPE: Microsoft Corporation
        PRESS: Enter

TYPE: One Microsoft Way
PRESS: [Enter]
TYPE: Redmond, WA 98052
PRESS: [Ctrl]+[Home]

b. To select the entire text area in the Notepad window:
PRESS: [Shift] and hold it down
PRESS: [Ctrl]+[End]
The entire text is highlighted.

c. To copy this information to the Clipboard:
CHOOSE: Edit, Copy
Notice that the information appears in the Clipboard Viewer window (Figure 5.8).

Figure 5.8

Copying information to the Clipboard

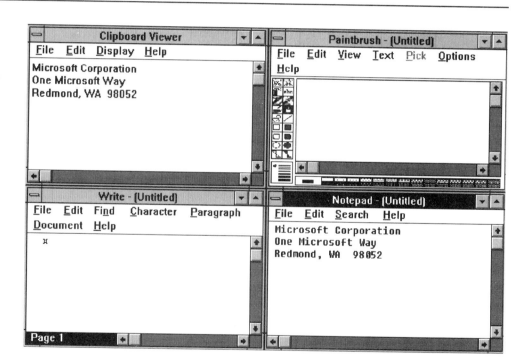

d. Select the Write application window.
e. CHOOSE: Edit, Paste
The information is inserted at the current cursor position in Write.
f. PRESS: [Enter] three times to insert some blank lines
g. Select the Paintbrush application window.
h. Moving the Brush tool like a pen, sign your name on the canvas.
i. Select the Pick tool (✂) from the Tool Box.

j. Starting at the top left-hand corner of your signature:
    CLICK: left mouse button and hold it down
    DRAG: mouse pointer to the bottom right-hand corner so that the
    rectangle surrounds the entire signature
    (Note: Do not include too much white space in the selection.)
k. Release the mouse button.
l. Copy the outlined graphic to the Clipboard:
    CHOOSE: Edit, Copy
    Notice that the graphic appears in the Clipboard Viewer.
m. Select the Write application window.
n. To embed the object into the Write document:
    CHOOSE: Edit, Paste Special
    SELECT: Paste command button
    The graphic appears in the document.
o. Select the Paintbrush application window.
p. Exit Paintbrush and do not save the graphic:
    CHOOSE: File, Exit
    SELECT: No command button
q. Select the Write application window, if it is not already selected.
r. Because embedded objects contain a link to the server application,
    you can edit the graphic in its original application:
    DOUBLE-CLICK: Signature object
    The Paintbrush application window appears for you to edit the
    object.
s. Add an underline to the signature.
t. CHOOSE: File, Exit & Return to (Untitled)
u. PRESS: [Enter] or CLICK: Yes to update the object in Write
    When you return to the Write application window, the signature has
    an underline.
v. Close all the open applications, except for Program Manager, and
    do not save the changes.
w. Exit Windows.

Windows 3.1

Index

Index